Refuse to Stay Broken

REFUSE TO STAY
BROKEN

A TRUE STORY OF GOD'S REDEEMING GRACE

by

Christina Stokesbury

Total Fusion Press
Strasburg, Ohio

Total Fusion Press
6475 Cherry Run Rd., Strasburg, OH 44680
www.totalfusionpress.com

Printed in the United States of America
24 23 22 21 20 19 18 17 16 15   1 2 3 4 5

ISBN-10: 194349603X
ISBN-13: 978-1-943496-03-7
Library of Congress Control Number: 2015918886

Editor: Andrea Long
Cover Creative Inspiration: Shaun Dillehay
Back Cover Photo: Serendipity Photography by Monica Washburn
Cover Art: Tirisa Edwards
Interior Layout: Kara Starcher

Some names and identifying details have been changed to protect the privacy of individuals.

Published in Association with Total Fusion Ministries, Strasburg, OH.
www.totalfusionministries.org

Dedication

*In Him we have redemption through His blood,
the forgiveness of sins, according to the riches of His grace.
Ephesians 1:7*

I praise the Lord for all He has done in my life and I dedicate this book, my story, and my life to Him—because without Him, I would still be nothing.

I made a lot of mistakes in life, but through the love of God I have been restored and made new. I am more than anything I could have ever dreamed of being. I have a wonderful husband that God gave me—a husband who is faithful and who loves me. I have three beautiful children here on earth and one in heaven—children that I love with my entire heart and who belong to God but are mine on loan.

God is my provider, my protector, and to Him I give all the glory. This book is His. I pray blessings and healing over all who read it. I pray for God to set people free through this book. I pray that His name will be glorified and that many will call upon Him because they see they can release the hurt, anger, and pain and grow into beauty and life with God.

Table of Contents

Foreword

It is one of my greatest honors and pleasures to introduce the author of this book. Chris Stokesbury is honestly one of the most gracious and amazing women I have encountered in my life. She has such a true talent for connecting with others, no matter the phase of the journey they are on. In my own journey, she has played so many valuable roles; Chris has been a friend, mentor, and a sister in time of need. I have had the pleasure of walking with her through many seasons of her own journey, and I can tell you that there is no one on this planet with a truer or more sincere heart for the health and welfare of others.

I was born into a very dysfunctional family and raised in a lifestyle with great conflicts. My mother was an alcoholic, and I eventually landed myself in prison at a young age through my own rebellion. When I chose to make positive decisions, I was released from prison. I decided to volunteer in the Department of Corrections, and this is where my path collided with Chris's. She inevitably became a driving force in my journey. We were initially paired together to facilitate a class called "Life's Healing Choices" for the Department of Corrections.

Chris and I are two women from very different lifestyles, yet we are very much alike. We come from very diverse backgrounds, yet connect on a level that is multi-faceted, including a deep spiritual connection. Because of her intensity of humility, I had no idea that I had just encountered the greatest mentor of my life. Throughout the years in my journey in overcoming life after incarceration and the loss of my family, Chris stepped in without hesitation or judgment and supported me emotionally, spiritually, and even financially at times. She became the family I had lost and poured her heart out to help me through the many trials I have had to face over the years since we met. Even through the many trials of her own that she has faced, she has proven to put the needs of others over her own and is an amazing mother and woman of grace and integrity.

When Chris first told me of this book and shared inside details of the motivation and writings, I became extremely excited. This book is definitely a best seller! I believe that the author will reach and encourage so many that are going through a diversity of struggles in their own lives. Spiritual warfare is a very dominant factor in the lives of us all, and Chris has a natural gifting in overcoming adversities through discipline and encouragement. May all be blessed by the wisdom and instruction that Chris has obtained through her own heartfelt journey to the pathway of peace and blessing.

Tammy Lozano
Recovery Support Specialist

Preface

When I was younger, I felt God telling me I would write a book. As I got older, the feeling became increasingly stronger. After I became involved in prison ministry, I knew it was time to write. We all have a story, and we must be willing to have the strength to share and heal. God doesn't want us to stay broken.

God allows things to take place in our lives for many reasons. Sometimes it is because of sin in this world or sin in our lives or simply to get our attention. However, with everything that happens, no matter how small or big, no matter what, God can use our stories to heal others as long as we allow healing in our own lives. First and foremost, we have to be obedient, love beyond all faults, and submit to God's will. Sometimes that is hard to do, especially when someone is as stubborn as I am! However, I have learned that in God all things can be beautiful. It's part of our inheritance as children of God.

Too many times in life I see people get hit with difficulties. They get blown to the ground by circumstances, sin, or choices they have made for themselves. What I see most in people who become broken is that they stay broken. They use their brokenness as an excuse for where they are in life or why they can't become more. Brokenness tends to define who they are as a person, and they never break free and allow healing to take place in their lives—full healing.

At times in our lives, either the world can take us to our

knees or God will. But either way, when we fall to our knees, God didn't create us to stay down but to stand back up. It's when we stay down that the darkness gets the better of us. We are to be the light of the world, and in order to light the world, we cannot allow hurt, pain, frustration, or anger darken our lives. We are to allow God to be the ruler.

As you read this book, you will see that I understand what it feels like to be broken. I may not know what you have gone through specifically, but I do know this: life hurts at times, and we can either allow the ups and downs in life to create us or we can allow them to destroy us. No matter what we are going through, it's our choice as to how we will respond and if we push forward to become more than what we see. It is healing to have another vision for ourselves over what we already know.

Through all of my brokenness in life, I found the only true life is in my Lord and Savior, my King, my Father, God. He was the one who took all of the destruction that was in my life and turned that to beauty. But to become beautiful, I had to be willing to lay it all down and give it all to Him. I had to say, "I don't know how to get through this, but with You, Father, all things are possible."

> And we know that all things work together for
> good to those who love God, to those who are
> the called according to His purpose.
> (Romans 8:28)

Romans 8:28 is my favorite verse because I do believe that God can and will create beauty out of all things, if we allow Him to. The key words in that verse are "to those who love God and are called." I refuse to stay broken because I am called to do more in my life. I am not called to sin and destruction; I am not called to stay in one place. I am called to be an overcomer, to be more than anything I could ever dream. That could be a successful business person, a full-time ministry worker, or just a faithful stay-at-home mom; whatever the call may be, I have to be willing to obey. Through obedience comes treasure.

Refuse to Stay Broken shows that even in our brokenness, God can create something amazing. However, we have to be willing to submit and hand it all over to God. We have to be willing to say, "I can't, but You can, Father." We have to be obedient to His call. With and through God, all of our brokenness can become beautiful.

*Note: Some names and details have been changed throughout this book to protect those involved. I am not here to condemn, as I am an imperfect sinner. I only included what was necessary to tell my story, to the glory of God, without harming others.

...for all have sinned and fall short
of the glory of God...
Romans 3:23

Christina Stokesbury

For more information, visit: www.ChrisStokesbury.com

Chapter One

Growing Up

I can do all things through Christ who strengthens me.
Philippians 4:13

Throughout my growing-up years, my mom instilled Philippians 4:13 into me. She wanted me to know that no matter the circumstance, no matter the step or the call, I could do all things through Christ. This verse has been a great encouragement in my life, and I hope you can find the same reassurance and strength in it.

Start at the Beginning

To understand a person through the trials of life, I think it is wise to know them from the very beginning. I was born in Oklahoma in 1977, and I grew up in a household with a single mother and an older brother. Probably the biggest influence in my life was my mother. I know many people may say that this is also true of themselves, but I believe that my mother was a true blessing in my life. Now that she is gone from this world and enjoying her heavenly home, I realize this truth even more and thank God continually for all that she did to train me up in God's Word and set my feet along His path. But, more about her later—it is time for you to meet me.

Following are little stories to let you know the personality I had growing up; I have always had a fun personality and try to make the best out of everything. I enjoyed school, not because of the learning portion, but rather everything that came with it. The year I graduated I was the president of student council, football homecoming queen, co-captain of the girls' basketball team, cheerleading captain, and captain of the volleyball team. I was laid-back and outgoing, and I loved pretty much everyone—exactly the person my mom raised me to be.

I went to the same school from kindergarten all the way through twelfth grade graduation. In kindergarten I met my first best friend, Holly, and to this day we can still call each other and talk as if we haven't skipped any time between our calls. She has been there through the thick and thin. We have gone through a lot together; we traveled together for school games; and, when her family went on trips, they took me with them at times.

Summer

As a kid, summer was, of course, always my favorite time. When I was old enough to stay home alone, I would climb onto the roof to lay out. When I did this, I would slather Crisco all over me to increase my tan. I even have a picture a neighbor took of me so she could show my mom what I was doing while my mom was at work. It's kind of funny, but, when I look back on it, kind of dumb as well. (If my kids are reading this, do not even think about getting onto our roof or tanning with Crisco!) I just figured the higher you get the better the tan, and what better way to tan than with Crisco? Yes, this was me: crazy and fun. I would try anything at least once, as long as it wasn't illegal or too dangerous.

On the rooftop. I am the one wearing the sunglasses.

Driving

Before I was a legal driver, one of my older cousins, Steve, tried to teach me how to drive. I was fourteen at the time, and I remember the night all too well. My cousin took me to a small empty church parking lot to drive a standard shift car instead of an automatic. The parking lot was just large enough for practicing. My driving was not pretty, and I have to admit I almost hit a pole, which happened to be the only pole in the entire parking lot.

Everything was going great, kind of, minus the jerking back

and forth every time I tried to go out of first gear. We were having fun and I was making progress, but everything changed for me the moment I noticed two cops sitting in a car, watching us from across the street. Mind you, I was fourteen and driving illegally without a parent in a parking lot in the middle of the city. The moment I noticed the cops, my heart started beating out of my chest, and I knew if I was caught driving at my age I would be in big trouble. After pointing out the cops to Steve, I asked him if we should switch places, but he felt that if we were to do that, we would look too suspicious, so he had me continue my lesson. The cops didn't come over, so we stayed in the parking lot practicing until it was dark—probably nine or ten at night.

Just when I thought we were clear, the cops came up behind us with their lights on. I stopped the car and waited anxiously for my punishment. When the officers got to our car, they then requested that we exit the car and put our hands above our heads. Not cool. While I complied with their request, I scanned through my panicked thoughts of what I was going to do. Then Steve started doing something that threw me for a loop. He started laughing at the cops. *What was he thinking?* I looked at him with terror. But, thank the LORD, the cops started laughing as well. *What was going on? Are they all going crazy?* Well, it turned out that the two cops that pulled us over were close friends of my cousin. They only pulled us over to play a prank because they realized who was in the car driving erratically in the church parking lot.

Protected

My mom was very protective but not a hovering parent. She usually let me do anything I requested as long as she knew where I was. I never had a curfew but that is because she trusted me and I never took advantage of that trust. If my mom told me to come home after an event, I would go home.

When I started driving, she bought me my first cell phone because I kept hitting things with my car and blowing my tires out. (I guess my driving didn't improve a whole lot!) I was the first kid in my school to have a cell phone, and back in my younger days, cell phones were boxes, big and heavy. Not too many people had cell phones, but because of my lack of driving skills, I needed a cell phone for my safety.

When I drove, I didn't pay a lot of attention to things around me. I pray my children are much better drivers then I was when I was younger! For instance, one day I was driving and eating a taco simultaneously when I dropped my taco in mid-turn. At this time of my life, losing a taco meant I would let go of the steering wheel to bend over and pick up the taco to resume the more important task of eating. That was the first time that I blew out both tires on my passenger side. It was pretty sad—I blew out so many tires that the guys at the tire store knew me by name.

The Big Banana

In high school my friends and I did what a lot of kids did— we toilet papered houses for fun. We never went halfway with our T.P. jobs, either. When I would drive the cheerleaders out to T.P., it never failed—I hit a trashcan or a curb, and one time we accidently drove up in someone's yard, running over their bushes. I'm sorry for all of it now.

I will have to say it was a true blessing that I drove a tank for my first car. I purchased the bulky Ford Granada from my grandma, and I was proud of that big banana. It was large, yellow, and a true tank. That car hit so many things and yet it kept on going like the Energizer Bunny. I even hit a cement block at the gas station once. That cement block put a pretty nice dent on the side of the car, but I was fine; thankfully, that cement block kept me from hitting the gas tanks. Thank you, Lord, again.

I bought the big banana with cash when I turned sixteen. I had waited tables all summer to earn the money to buy my car. By the end of summer I had enough money to pay cash for that tank. Of course, it helped that my grandma sold the car to me for way cheaper than she should have—it was garage kept and in perfect condition when I bought it. In fact, it only had 1,300 miles the day I drove it home!

My Ford Granada. Oh, you had to love Fords back then! That engine would be shaking and rattling long after it had been turned off and the key taken out. I'd have to walk away from a car that was still moving with nobody in it. That was embarrassing, especially being young when you're trying to be cool!

After owning that car I swore I would never buy a Ford again, but we have an F-150 now, and I actually love that truck. My brother had a Ford Tempo that lasted forever, my mom owned a Ford Sable that she loved and it lasted forever, but nothing beats my mom's car she had when we were young. It was a huge green Ford car that my brother and I called "The Booger Machine." The Booger Machine would smoke and backfire as we drove down the road—yes, we were that family. We would laugh so hard and hide in the floorboards because it was so embarrassing. Of course, everything changed when my mom kept getting promoted with the government. She eventually bought a car that was nice, and, yes, she paid cash for the new car. We never bought anything if we couldn't pay for it in full. My mom believed that you don't buy cheap because you get what you pay for, but you do shop around and find the best deal.

Football Homecoming Queen -
Despite the embarassing car!

Chapter Two

My Mom, My Hero

Train up a child in the way he should go,
And when he is old he will not depart from it.
Proverbs 22:6

My mom was a faithful, loving woman of God, but things were not always easy for our family. Through a lot of fire, testing, and training, she came to the realization that God truly is in control and that His Word is true. Her faith shaped our family and, in turn, my own life in Christ.

You see, my mom experienced a great trial: ten days before I was born, her husband of thirteen years left her. The day he left, he said he was going on a camping trip only to call *on her birthday* (three days before the day of my birth) to say he wasn't coming home. At that time, this call understandably left my mom helpless and afraid and in great despair. She even told me when I was older that if it weren't for my brother and me, she would have taken her own life; however, she said she didn't follow through because she knew we needed her. I believe it was the grace and protection of God that she didn't take her life.

Hidden Blessings

Ironically, what seemed so terrible at the time turned out to be a blessing. The day my father, Roy, left was the day God rescued our family. Even though it didn't seem like a rescue at the time, God continued to reveal His plan and purpose in our lives throughout the years. We were called to a purpose.

> And we know that all things work together for good to those who love God, to those who are called according to *His* purpose. (Romans 8:28)

> For many are called, but few *are* chosen. (Matthew 22:14)

My mom was a stay-at-home mom to a three-year-old little boy the day Roy left. She had no money or means of making money, as she was without a job or training. With all of the odds working against her, she had one major blessing in her favor, and that was God. Despite her own despair, she continued to faithfully raise us in a godly home and provide for us in whatever ways she could.

> A father of the fatherless, a defender of widows, *Is* God in His holy habitation. (Psalm 68:5)

While my mother was truly amazing, I still grew up with a lot of hurt from not having a fatherly figure around. I never knew what it was like to have an actual, physical dad hug me, say he loved me, buy me presents, give me birthday cards, or even tell me that I made him proud. When I was young, I yearned for this earthly father, but I am thankful today that I always had my heavenly Father. My heavenly Father might not have hugged me *physically*, but He has held me many times and has carried me through a lot. He might not have bought me presents, but He has given me way more than I deserve. My heavenly Father might not have said, "I am proud of you," but I know His love is sufficient for all of my needs. I was blessed to have an amazing mom who knew to teach me that God is my Father, and this was one of the best lessons in life I could have ever learned as a child.

First Meeting

The first time I ever met Roy was at a funeral when I was eleven years old. I remember that day someone came up to me at the funeral and said, "Oh, you must be Roy's daughter." The moment that statement was made, my anger rose up, and my reply was "Yes, he is my biological father, but not my dad." I was so hurt by him for missing out on my life and leaving my mother alone. Later when I was thirteen years old, we went out to meet him and took a picture with him, but all I remember is that he bought me a stuffed dog because I guess my mom told him that was what I liked at the time.

Fatherhood

I had no contact with Roy when I was young so I never really knew him before my mom passed away. I only knew what my mom told me and what his family told me. Since my mom's passing, he has come around a few times, and at least he tries. He is very nervous and can't stay in one place long. He isn't good with a lot of people, and he seems on edge. I was told it was from things he witnessed and went through in the Vietnam War and that he wasn't like that before his service. He recently called to tell me he was sorry, that he wasn't trying to leave me, but he never left the war. He wanted to say more, but that in itself was a big step for him, and I was proud of him. I don't hold anything against him; my heart has forgiven everything, but I still can't really look to him as a daughter does her father. I do care about him, but he is just a part of my life, not in my life. My true Father is the one I grew up with, and that is my Father in heaven. He is the one I could talk to anytime, and He was there at all times.

When my mom passed away, Roy and his wife started making their way into my life. For this I am glad because I have been able to overcome some hurt through our reconciliation. I never was angry with him because I know he had been through a lot in the Vietnam War, but I still had hurt that needed to heal. I don't consider him my dad as if I know him and grew up with him, but I refer to him as simply Roy, someone I know and care about.

One day when I was speaking at a church giving my testimony, Roy's wife showed up to hear me speak. Because my story included Roy, I started crying thinking about how she would respond. However, she did the exact opposite of what I expected—she came and hugged me, and then she opened up about her past. This is when I realized that we are all broken somewhere. My heart went out to her, and I knew she was now in my life for a reason, even if it is just to pray for her. She has a place in my heart that she doesn't know, all because of that one night when I saw who she was and how she had overcome, but still had some hurt—a hurt that would be hard to heal unless God was doing the healing.

I used to blame Roy for leaving, but I don't anymore. It took growing up to see that the Vietnam War really did change him, and as I get older, I see how bad any war can affect anyone involved. Now, I have a heart for my earthly father. I feel sorry for his suffering, I thank him for his service, and I pray for him and his wife. I want the best for them, and I pray blessings into their life and marriage.

God's Will, Our Prayers

Sadly, my mom is no longer with me today—she's gone on to her heavenly home. But when she was alive, I remember her telling me that before Roy left her, she said a prayer that she believed changed the entire dynamics of our family. Her prayer and desire was to have a godly family—a family who lived their lives for God. Well, God answered her prayers, although not in the way she thought He would. Roy leaving paved the way for us to lean more fully on Christ and trust in His Word and timing, shaping us into the godly family that my mother desired. You see, God does answer prayers, but not always in our timing or desires.

> Delight yourself also in the Lord, And He shall
> give you the desires of your heart. (Psalm 37:4)

Many believers misinterpret this verse by believing that, if they love the Lord, they will get everything they desire or pray for, but that is not its purpose. This verse is basically instructing us to delight in the Lord, and when we do, our hearts will desire what His heart is for our own lives. When our desires become His, He will fulfill those desires, because at that time our hearts work in unison with His. This is why many who pray for things that are within their own hearts' desire fail or face rejection. They get flustered as to why God isn't answering their prayers—but it is necessary to desire what God desires. My mom did this, and it caused her great temporary grief—but an eternal reward. A great example of this is when Jesus was praying in the Garden of Gethsemane, He said, "Father, please take this cup from me, but only if it is Your will." Even Jesus himself desired God's will over his own.

This is also why many believers who are awesome Christians will pray to win the lottery and not win. They may even wish to use the money for ministry or give it all away, and yet their request is still refused. Their prayer and desire may be pure and true, but maybe it is not God's plan for their life. When we walk in His plan, our heart changes—we get to where we don't care if we win. All we care about is serving the Lord and doing His will in our lives. Not that anyone would complain about actually winning the lottery, but when we desire His heart, we become humbled to God and His purpose in our life.

God knew what was to be done and what was to take place in my mom's life before the knowledge was ever given to her. It wasn't that we couldn't be a godly home with Roy there; it was that he wasn't in the state of mind to be involved in the plan that God had for us.

Forgiving

My mom always taught me to forgive, and she never wanted me to hold any grudges, even against my dad.

> [14] For if you forgive men their trespasses, your heavenly Father will also forgive you. [15] But if you do not forgive men their trespasses, neither will your Father forgive your trespasses. (Matthew 6:14-15)

This verse is very powerful if you think about it. It's almost scary—if we hold any grudges or unforgiveness in our lives, we will not be forgiven of our own sins. When I was young, this never resonated with me, but as I have gotten older, God has taught me the true meaning of forgiveness on both ends. My God, my Father, cannot forgive me if I don't forgive others. That means forgiving my neighbor even when they irritate me. It means praying for someone when I would rather curse them. It means forgiving even my earthly father.

My mom would always say, "Don't let one person keep you

from heaven." Man, that is a powerful statement! I never really understood what she meant when she would tell me that. I would just acknowledge the statement but not accept it within because it wasn't made clear to me yet. Now that I know, it speaks volumes to me about forgiveness.

My mom was wise beyond her years. I cannot recall her ever being mean or talking bad about people. Even when she spoke about Roy leaving, she never said anything bad about him. She forgave and raised us to forgive. She also raised us in church. Every Sunday morning and Wednesday night, we went to church that was held in other people's homes. I went to a Christian school and everyone who went there went to big churches; none of my friends had ever heard of church in the home. Sadly, a couple of my friends believed I was in a cult because of the home church. My reply to this misconception was always that "Yes, we get together and listen to the Word of God, and we believe in God. We aren't a denomination. We just believe in a deep meaning of His Word, which is not just black and white—it's deep, it's spiritual. We believe in a relationship, and that's really all that matters in the end." Even my best friend growing up wasn't allowed to go to church with me.

I have to admit that I didn't like church at all growing up. I remember that while sitting in service, I would draw, daydream, play, and do everything but listen. Now that I am older I see that even though I didn't think I was listening, my spirit was. The things I heard growing up in service have stuck with me throughout life. God is good.

Growing Up

After I was born, my mom was blessed with a job working for the government. When she started this, her first adult job, she was a secretary but ended up being promoted again and again to the highest level possible without education during her working years before she was blessed with early retirement. For a single mother with no work experience, she really excelled and was blessed in return throughout her career.

During her years here on this earth, she kept her priorities in this strict order: God, her family, then work. She was so selfless, always putting us above herself—even though that meant never dating because her time was spent working hard to put my brother and me through Christian school and then spending her free time going to our games and activities. She wanted us to have the childhood she never had, and because of that, we were allowed to play every sport we ever wanted. My brother played football and basketball. I played basketball, volleyball, soccer, and participated in cheerleading all through my school years (when the option was available).

Through all these seasons and years of sports, my mom only missed one of my games and that was only because of my own stubborn foolishness. Earlier that day we had an argument in which I told her I didn't want her to be at my game. I regretted those words the minute they left my mouth, but I was so angry about whatever we were fighting about (I can't even remember now) that I stuck to my guns. During the entire game that night, I looked for my mom, wishing that she would show up, but she never did.

He who guards his mouth preserves his life,
But he who opens wide his lips shall have destruction. (Proverbs 13:3)

My mom proved a point the day she didn't go to my game.
Our words are powerful; they can speak life or death, healing or sickness, heaven or hell. I learned that day that I needed to be careful with what I said because you can never take
back spoken words. Our words flow from our hearts. If we
keep our hearts pure, all that comes forth will be uplifting
and wholesome to the ears and hearts of others. I pray this
blessing on your own life today, Amen!

Being strong in the sight of others was a big deal to me, because in my eyes, my mom was strong. She was my hero, and
in so many ways, I wanted to be like her. During her life, I

only saw her cry a few times, and when she did cry, it was because she was afraid of how she was going to pay bills. Even though she cried, she was always careful to not cry in front of us—she never wanted us to fear or to not trust God. She always said, "God will provide," and He always did.

By the time my brother and I entered junior high and high school, my mom was making enough money for us to be considered upper-middle class, and because of the training, trials, and tribulation my mom went through in the early years of having us, she was ready for the blessings God gave. She never took advantage of having money, but always paid cash, never putting herself in debt. She also never took advantage of the love God had and gave freely to us. She was always grateful and praised God all the way to the end of this life.

Reap What You Sow

> [7] Do not be deceived, God is not mocked; for whatever a man sows, that he will also reap. [8] For he who sows to his flesh will of the flesh reap corruption, but he who sows to the Spirit will of the Spirit reap everlasting life. [9] And let us not grow weary while doing good, for in due season we shall reap if we do not lose heart. (Galatians 6:7-9)

Treat people the way you want to be treated because you reap what you sow. Now, if I had walked in this at all times, that would have made for a wonderful life. Unfortunately, I have had plenty of moments where I wish I had been kinder. These were the times where I stepped up and spoke before thinking about what was coming out. If only everyone in the world lived by the motto "Think before you speak", a lot of the hurt that takes place wouldn't exist, more people would look wiser than what they are, and bullies wouldn't be such an issue in schools.

I remember many times when my mom was treated harshly due to her weight. My whole life, she was overweight but did not deserve to be treated less than others because of her outward appearance. She used to tell me, "Never let yourself get overweight; people are not as nice to you when you are." I used to tell her that couldn't be true, but I noticed many times where my mom would be hurt from the way people acted around her.

> [1] Judge not, that you be not judged. [2] For with what judgment you judge, you will be judged; and with the measure you use, it will be measured back to you. [3] And why do you look at the speck in your brother's eye, but do not consider the plank in your own eye?"
> (Matthew 7:1-3)

> "...For *the Lord does* not *see* as man sees; for man looks at the outward appearance, but the Lord looks at the heart." (1 Samuel 16:7b)

Heroes Can Be Broken, Too

One time when my mom, my boyfriend, and I all went out to eat, we were sitting at a table next to some unkind people who were laughing and making jokes about my mom. The jokes were loud enough for us to hear. I remember looking over at my mom to see her eyes tearing up, and that broke me. I learned in that moment that my mom isn't a superhero, she can be broken, and this world can be a cruel place. She never said anything to the other table, nor did I at the time because I knew the extra attention would only make matters worse by embarrassing her further. However, when she left minutes before I walked out the door, I made sure to have a word with the rude table about their manners.

Because of the way I grew up, I don't take kindly to people who make fun of others, especially those who are overweight. I don't appreciate the "fat" word. Even though I may be guilty of calling myself just that from time to time, I would never allow another person to say such a harsh word in my home. People have to understand that when they speak rudely about others, they will in the end reap what they sow.

> ...but, speaking the truth in love, may grow
> up in all things into Him who is the head—
> Christ... (Ephesians 4:15)

Anyone who knew my mom would say that she lit up the room. She had a smile that would make anyone smile, and she was beautiful inside and out. It was her joyful spirit—she was full of life and it showed through to everyone.

> "The lamp of the body is the eye. If therefore
> your eye is good, your whole body will be full
> of light." (Matthew 6:22)

Pieces of My Heart

My mom and I were best friends. She was there when I needed her; she was even there when I didn't think I needed her. We shared everything, but she kept one thing from me that I didn't find out until years after she had passed. She didn't ever tell us that my dad signed over his parental rights. I knew he didn't pay child support, but I had no clue he gave us up entirely. I guess she never wanted us to feel rejected, hurt, angry, or sad over the situation. She did everything to protect us and show us love, no matter what the cost was to her. She showed love and she shined in love in everything she did.

Many times I think back about the times I took her for granted, the times I wish I could change. If I could change things, I would in a heartbeat. Now it's too late, she is gone, and all I can do is say that I love her and I wish I could show her now how much she is and was loved. The saying "You never know what you have until it is gone" is so true. I knew I had an awesome mom, but I didn't realize how amazing she really was until she was gone.

Don't take love, family, life or anyone for granted because you never know when they could be gone. You never know when the last kiss or last hug could be, so savor every minute you have with your parents, grandparents, children, husband, wife, and those who you know you can't live without.

My mother, Joyce Elaine Cobb
Photo taken in 1965

Don't take advantage, and don't hold on to anger. Forgive and walk in forgiveness.

A good parent isn't defined by what they can give. A good parent is defined by their love, their actions, their faith, their patience, and their honesty. My mom was the best parent I could have ever asked for from God. If you are a parent, rest in knowing that God chose you for the specific purpose of raising your specific children and that you are enough for them. In His grace, someday they will realize all you did for them and be grateful. God is good.

Chapter Three

Learning the Hard Way

"Fear not, for I am with you;
Be not dismayed, for I am your God.
I will strengthen you, Yes, I will help you,
I will uphold you with My righteous right hand."
Isaiah 41:10

In September of 1995, I was a tender eighteen years old when I started dating a friend of my cousin's. I was at a restaurant called The Kettle studying for a college test late one night when a man walked up to introduce himself—his name was Roberto. That night I actually ended up leaving early to get away from him because I knew something didn't feel right during our first meeting. Later I received a call from my cousin Steve who just happened to be at the same restaurant that night when Roberto came up to visit with me. When Steve called me, it wasn't for anything but to give his approval of Roberto and to tell me that his friend really wanted to take me out on a date. Steve begged for me to give his friend a chance. I (being weak-minded and nice) told him one date, but that was it.

Our first date was set to occur at the same place we originally met, The Kettle. We were to meet at 7:00, but 7:00 came and went, and I was about to leave when the waitress came up to me and asked if I was waiting for Roberto. I was not amused and said, "Yes, but not anymore." She then proceeded to tell me that Roberto had called and was begging that I please wait, that he was on his way. His story for being late was that he left the iron on and he had to go back to unplug it. The waitress seemed to know Roberto well, and during our conversation, she gave approval of him as well. When he finally showed up, I was seconds from leaving, and to this day I wish I would have left, but I listened to everyone and gave him a chance.

We are to learn from our mistakes, or at least we should try to learn from each and every mistake. Sometimes it takes making the same mistake over and over before getting it straight; sometimes we don't ever get it right until we are at our deathbed. But if we are walking in Christ, He will protect and grow us up.

> And no wonder! For Satan himself transforms himself into an angel of light.
> (2 Corinthians 11:14)

> He shall cover you with His feathers, And under His wings you shall take refuge; His truth *shall be* your shield and buckler.
> (Psalm 91:4)

Now, I am not saying that Roberto was a devil, but when someone isn't walking for the Lord, the devil can easily use others to get to us. He comes to break us down, to bring us out of our covering. My new friend I met that night was suave, and he had a demeanor about him that was strong as well as confident. Roberto was of Italian decent with a medium build, black hair, and brown eyes. He was also a bit older than me—about twenty-six years old. He dressed in nice expensive clothing, and he drove a car that was well-kept. He had an accent that was beautiful, and he spoke three languages. He seemed intelligent, and he had a gift to talk his way through anything. Roberto had every waitress wrapped around his finger and anything he wanted he knew how to get.

After our first date he seemed to have weaseled his way into my life. I believed his stories even though my gut (God within) was telling me to stay clear of him—something drew me to him. I now know that the attraction was by no means leading from God.

> Put on the whole armor of God, that you may
> be able to stand against the wiles of the devil.
> (Ephesians 6:11)

God tells us to put on our armor, to protect ourselves against the attacks of the enemy. I know this man I dated wasn't what God had intended for me, but when you aren't walking fully in Christ, it's easier to fall into sin than to obey what the Father is telling us. God gives clear warnings when we aren't living in obedience to Him.

"So then, because you are lukewarm, and neither cold nor hot, I will vomit you out of My mouth." (Revelation 3:16)

Dating Life

I started dating this suave guy, even though everything within me was saying no. He would take me to clubs and places that I was way too young to go to, but somehow he was able to get me into every place we ever went, with no questions asked. Everywhere Roberto took me, everyone knew him like he was a celebrity, and he seemed to hold his own as if he were. He would even get on stages in public places and sing to me in front of everyone—this guy had a voice that could melt any heart. It was odd but I started noticing that I had fallen under his spell that seemed to be over every lady at every place we visited. I don't know if it was his accent, his demeanor, the way he treated me with such class, or the way he gave and spoiled me with everything I wanted.

No matter how good he seemed to be, I still knew in my heart something was off. A year of dating went by, and during that time, I was wined and dined, and all seemed great. My mom loved him, and he was good to me, but I started catching onto things he would say and how he would take care of things that made me worry. I started catching him in lie after lie to the point of not knowing what to believe anymore.

During the year we were together, he would talk about how some things were best left unsaid, so he wouldn't tell me about his days. I didn't know what was the truth or a lie anymore; I never liked liars. I always told him to be honest, never cheat, and our relationship would work out. However, he started to show a trend I wasn't sure I wanted to be around. Roberto was still being good to me, and he was always there when I needed him, so I held onto him a little longer.

The Unforgettable Date

I was dressed to the hilt being taken out as usual, although this date in particular is one I won't ever forget. We went to an elegant restaurant, which had a male worker who went around and serenaded women. Unfortunately, this male singer decided to serenade me this evening. He sang in a language I didn't understand, but it sounded beautiful. After he sang to me, he then gave me a rose. During the song, I kept looking up at Roberto who had disapproval written all over him—in fact, he was on fire with anger. When I asked him what was wrong, I realized that he understood the words to the song that was being sung to me. However, the guy who serenaded me had no clue that my boyfriend could speak other languages. Roberto then began to tell me what the song was about. After he explained the song, I knew exactly why he wasn't too happy. When Roberto was done explaining, he then dismissed himself from the table for a few minutes. I didn't see the guy who serenaded me the rest of the night. I am not sure if he left or if my boyfriend had a talk with him—who knows—all I know is Roberto was upset about the song and upset with me as if it was my fault.

On the way home from the date, Roberto was still mad about the entire thing that took place at the restaurant. He was so angry he started blurting out things that were unacceptable in my vocabulary; one sentence in particular changed our entire relationship. He yelled, "If you ever leave me, I will bury your body so deep that nobody will ever find you!" Talk about throwing me for a loop. I told him right then to pull over and let me out, I didn't trust him, and I didn't want to be in the car or anywhere near him for that matter. He continued to drive and wouldn't pull over, nor would he let me out, so I ended up letting myself out. This was the first, and hopefully only time, I will ever have to jump out of a moving car. Mind you, I had a dress and heels on making my leap and subsequent landing even trickier.

Walking Home

As I was limping home in my heels, Roberto followed in the car with the passenger window down. He kept yelling, "I am sorry, Christina. Get back in the car. Please, get back in the car."

Of course, I was so upset and not acting like my normal self that I told him not-so-gracefully to leave. I wanted nothing to do with him. He kept shouting, "Come on, Christina! You know I would never hurt you!" The begging didn't stop, and I didn't get back in the car.

It was almost sad now that I think back about the entire scene. I remember a man and his wife drove up and asked if I needed help—a ride or did I want them to call the police? I told them I was okay and that I was almost home, so no need. The man was worried; I am not sure if he saw the entire fiasco of a young girl jumping out of a moving vehicle or not. If he had, I am sure he would have called the police anyway, so I assume he didn't since no police arrived at the scene.

Persistence Pays Off

I eventually got home to my own room and locked the door. I was done with Roberto, and I wanted nothing to do with him. He arrived to speak with my mom, and after he left, she came to my room and asked what was wrong. I simply told her, "Nothing." I didn't tell her what he said, and now that I think back, I never ended up telling her about him threatening me.

Weeks went by, and Roberto kept coming to the house with roses or cards, anything just to get me to talk to him. Finally after both he and my mom kept bugging me about giving him another chance, I gave him one last chance and only one chance. After speaking with him, I told him that if he ever made me feel uncomfortable or threatened me again that I was gone and gone for good.

Back to Abnormal

Everything went back to our version of normal, or so it seemed. Even though I was very fit and in shape, I had high blood pressure every time I went to see my doctor. The doctor said that my blood pressure being high didn't make sense because I never had an issue before. When asked about what was going on in my life, I explained the situation with Roberto and even then the doctor said, "You need to get rid of that boyfriend or he is going to kill you." I knew that what the doctor was telling me was true in every way, but I didn't take any action on the subject yet, nor did I know even where to begin. I knew that if I left, he wouldn't let me go easily.

My birthday time rolled around and I started to feel a little suspicious about some things that Roberto was doing. The day of my birthday, I ended up going on a date with him but I had him take me home early, because something was off. I can't remember why I was feeling so strangely, but I do remember that I had decided it was time I found out what was going on when he wasn't with me, because I knew something was up that I wasn't going to like. I ended up calling one of my best friends to see if she wanted to hang out. She came over, and from there, "we took a drive." This is the phrase my mom and I used when we would go spy. My mom taught me to spy, and even though it was for a good purpose, it really wasn't a good lesson. However, I love everything my mom taught me, and now it is a memory I can look back on fondly.

Time to Spy

After going by four places that were Roberto's favorite spots, we finally found his car at a bar in Edmond. The workers at the bar knew me, so I knew I wouldn't have any issues getting in; but I didn't want to go in because I didn't want to be seen. My goal was to see what Roberto was doing and then leave, basically catch him in the act, whatever that was. As I was coming around the corner, I stood back behind a wall and peeked around the corner. What I noticed didn't seem to shock me at all: he was sitting at the bar with a girl on each side of him. As he was sitting there, he leaned over and whispered in one of the girl's ears. That was it, all the evidence I needed; I was truly done this time. It's sad that a death threat didn't do the trick but a whisper in another girl's ear did. This really shows my age and how much I needed to grow up.

> When I was a child, I spoke as a child, I understood as a child, I thought as a child; but when I became a man, I put away childish things.
> (1 Corinthians 13:11)

I was walking away and almost to the car when Roberto came running out of the bar. How he knew I was there, I am not sure, but I told him it was over—but for him it wasn't.

Physical

I arrived home around one in the morning. My mom was asleep and I locked the front door. As I was walking to my room, Roberto rang the doorbell. Of course, I didn't answer the door because I had nothing else I wanted to say to him. However, Roberto kept on ringing the doorbell, so I went and barely opened the door to tell him to leave, that my mom was sleeping, and what he was doing was rude.

The moment I opened the door Roberto pulled me out of the house by my arm, yanking me so hard it jerked my neck causing instant dizziness. Then he started yelling at me, and of course I wasn't one to hold back, so I yelled in return. He wasn't used to women standing up to him and this infuriated him. He shoved me so hard my head flew forward and popped my neck. I lost my composure for a moment and was even dizzier than I was before.

Once I came to a point where I could pull myself back together, I turned around, ran inside the house, and locked him out. He started yelling and ringing the doorbell again. This is when I finally decided to go get my mom.

Momma Bear

I went to my mom's room and woke her up. I flipped on the light and said, "Mom, look what he just did," showing her my arm which was covered in marks from where Roberto had grabbed me. My mom jumped out of bed, pulled the shotgun out of her closet, and went to the front door. My mom was far from being violent—she never raised her voice at me, she never yelled, she always held herself with grace, she never cussed, and she never spoke ill of others. The moment someone hurt her baby, she held that shotgun with authority, and that shocked me to the point that my mouth dropped open.

Roberto was still standing out on the porch trying to get me to come out of the house. It was now my time to sit back and let Mom take care of the problem. I sat in the living room when my mom went out the front door. I couldn't hear everything, but I did hear her tell him that if he ever put a hand on me again that he wouldn't see the light of day ever again. Man, my mom was awesome! I could hear him apologizing and begging my mom to forgive him. My mom came back in, and he left.

Stalking

After that night with my mom's support, I never went back to Roberto—praise God! However, for four years after that night, he stalked me. When I would leave my home, I would have flowers waiting on my car or little presents by the driver's side door. He waited for me throughout my relationship with another boyfriend, threatening that man's life, and the stalking even continued into my first year of marriage with my first husband.

> "No weapon formed against you shall prosper, And every tongue *which* rises against you in judgment You shall condemn. This *is* the heritage of the servants of the Lord, And their righteousness *is* from Me," Says the Lord. (Isaiah 54:17)

Chapter Four

Close Call

God is our refuge and strength,
A very present help in trouble.
Psalm 46:1

I went to a pediatrician until I was eighteen years old; one day I realized I was the oldest person in the waiting room. Before then I never knew there were doctors for children and doctors for adults. Pretty sad, I know—my husband jokingly calls it private school training. I just call it my "Chris bubble."

I often fought strep throat or tonsillitis when I was young. It really wasn't fun having your throat hurt all of the time, but I got used to it. I even played some basketball games with strep; of course, I was on antibiotics when I played. I got to the point where I had to live with it or I wasn't living.

Even though my tonsils were really bad, my pediatrician never believed in removing tonsils, no matter the circumstances. His rule was "God put them there for a reason." I believe that could be the case for some things, but if you had tonsils that were so scarred up and damaged like mine, you would know that it was worse to keep them than to remove them. I was later told that my tonsils were so bad and damaged from when I had mononucleosis that they were poisoning my body daily.

Finding a Doctor

While I was looking for a new doctor, I ended up going to one that was recommended to me by one of my mom's friends. I went to see Dr. Smith and thought he was nice but soon realized it was a mistake. He was a little too nice and touchy. When visiting him, he would rub on my inner thighs, and, of course, that always made me feel weird and uncomfortable, but I kept blowing it off as him being a friendly-touchy person. He also did a breast exam every time I went in to see him.

Unfortunately, I didn't know that what he was doing was inappropriate; I thought that maybe this was how the doctors for adults acted or conducted their practice. I know I was very naïve. I continued to see him for awhile, not feeling fully comfortable with him, but I didn't know any better. I lived in my "Chris bubble" where the whole world was nice and nothing could go wrong. Again, so little did I know back then.

Surgery Time

Despite my misgivings, at least Dr. Smith agreed that it was finally time to get my tonsils removed. I was nineteen years old and scared, but I knew my tonsils needed to be removed. This surgery was my first, so I didn't know what to expect. Everything seemed to go fine, but even though this was only the first of many subsequent surgeries in my life, it ranked at being the top of one of my worst experiences ever, one that almost took my life.

The surgery I went through took longer than what was expected. The doctor had to dig into the muscle in my neck due to scar tissue caused by repeat throat infections and mononucleosis when I was younger. This was very painful, and it caused the process of healing to take much longer.

I was a week post-surgery and out of pain medicine. I remember my mom taking me to Walgreens to get my prescription refilled, but I was in so much pain I couldn't remember anything except tears running down my face. Years later, when I was in that same Walgreens, a lady recognized me and told me that she saw me that day; she said that God had her pray for me, and she also stated that she was so glad to see I was okay. Thank you, Jesus, for the prayers and protection. I certainly needed them.

> ...praying always with all prayer and supplication in the Spirit, being watchful to this end with all perseverance and supplication for all the saints...(Ephesians 6:18)

Two weeks after surgery I still couldn't talk. I would write things on paper for my mom to know what I wanted or needed. It was miserable, but my misery did not seem to be an emergency; however, one night everything changed. I remember my mom was taking a bath, and I had to spit something out of my mouth that didn't taste right.

When I spit, blood was in the spit, and I immediately felt frightened. I ran into the bathroom where my mom was in the tub, and I gave her a piece of paper that read: "I just spit blood. Call the doctor and see if this is normal."

Mom looked at the paper and then took the phone I handed her. She called Dr. Smith immediately, but his response was "Yes, this is okay, just put ice on her throat."

Well, I started to ice, but I spit again and again. Each time I would spit, more blood was in the spit than the time before. I finally went to the mirror and looked into my throat. In the back of my throat, I saw what appeared to be a blood clot, so I ran to my mom with a new piece of paper: "I think there is a blood clot in the back of my throat." Then I gave her a flashlight to look for herself.

It had been thirty minutes since my mom had spoken with Dr. Smith, and I was still spitting blood and more blood than before. My mom called the doctor back, and he told her once again to keep ice on it, that my throat was just swollen, and that there was no blood clot in the back of my throat.

Ten more minutes went by, and my throat was continually getting worse. At this point my mom tried to call the doctor again, but he didn't answer; I guess he was tired of hearing from us and it was late. After my mom hung up the phone, she told me to get in the car; we were going to the hospital. Thank God we left when we did!

I took a cup with me so I could spit the blood into the cup so I wouldn't gag. We were halfway to the hospital when the spit turned into full-blown blood pouring out of my mouth. When the blood flow started, I had to bend over the cup and keep my mouth open so that I could breathe over the large lumps in the back of my throat. Even so, it was almost impossible to breathe over all of the blood coming out of my mouth.

This was the first time I had to say my last prayers. My mom was flying through stop light after stop light, and I could do nothing but silently say one last time, "God, forgive me of all of my sins." I knew I was going to die, and there was nothing we could do.

At the Hospital

My mom pulled up to the doors and told me to run. I got out covered in my own blood, still holding the cup that was now overflowing red. I went running in with my face down, because if I looked up I would start to choke on the blood that was coming out.

The moment I got into the hospital I ran up to the lady who was standing behind the counter. My head was in a downward position, but I had my eyes lifted so I could see her. The moment I got to her, she looked at me, she threw her hands up and everything she had in her hands went flying in the air. She took off running away from me. This was it. I knew I was dead; even the emergency room nurse was running from me. I looked behind me and all I could see was a trail of blood, pooling all around me.

As soon as I turned back around, the nurse was running toward me with two doctors and another nurse. They immediately rushed me to a room where they grabbed a tube and started suctioning my throat. They didn't know my name, nor did they know what had happened to me. They just knew that I was suffocating and about to bleed to death.

The suction was horrible. Trying to breathe over the blood clots in my throat, the flowing blood, and the tube they were using to suction my throat was just not working. I started gagging, so I pushed one doctor off of me so I could bend over to try to breathe. I remember them throwing me back into the chair and holding me down saying, "We have to do this." I had one doctor and two nurses holding me down while the other doctor was shoving this thing down my throat. I was fighting them, but not because I was trying to defy what they were doing—I was just trying to breathe.

As I was sitting in the chair, I remember feeling helpless like nothing was going to save my life, and then it happened. One clot came out. At this point the doctor was trying to see in my throat and that's when he realized I had more clots, so he grabbed some forceps and reached into my throat, pulling two more rather large clots out of my throat. Oh, thank you, God! I could breathe.

They sprayed something into my throat to help stop the bleeding. Only when it began to slow could the doctors find out my name and information from my mom who had finally arrived in the room with us.

My mom explained everything to them, and when they found out this was the caused by a tonsillectomy, they were furious. The emergency doctor said whoever did my surgery had cut something in the back of my throat that caused a slow leak of blood that ended up rupturing when the clots became too much. When my mom told him that our doctor wouldn't answer our last call, the doctor at the hospital took it upon himself to call Dr. Smith. I was told the ER doctor gave Dr. Smith an earful, but I'm not sure. Remember this was years ago when they weren't so confidential, nor did they worry about disclosing information in fear of being taken to court. This was a time that if you wanted to know something, you were told.

Finally I was able to lie down in the emergency room. I had lost so much blood that I had no strength in my body left to sit up or walk. As I was lying there, I remember the doctor telling my mom that we might have to go back into surgery. The moment I heard that is when I started praying, "No, God, no more surgery!"

Miracles Happen

My throat quit bleeding. I was ordered to bed rest due to the blood loss, but, crazy enough, after this was taken care of, my throat started feeling better and I was able to start talking again. No more surgery would be required.

> "...by stretching out Your hand to heal, and that
> signs and wonders may be done through the
> name of Your holy Servant Jesus." (Acts 4:30)

A few days after my hospital visit, Dr. Smith called to see me for a follow-up. The day I went in to see him was the last day I saw that doctor. Not because of the mistake he made with my throat, because mistakes happen; nor was it because he blew us off—it was pretty late, and he didn't realize the severity of the issue. It was because of one thing he did and one thing he said during my visit.

When Dr. Smith came into the room, the first thing he said was "The guys in the surgery room all thought you were pretty." My stomach turned at that moment and I started to feel uncomfortable. After he looked at my throat and after doing my entire checkup, he said, "Well, I will see you next time." As he said this, he put his hands on my cheeks and then he leaned forward to kiss me. Now I know people are friendly, but come on. I know doctors are not supposed to kiss their patients. As soon as I realized what he was doing ,I turned my head and he got my cheek.

I left there thinking "This can't be normal." My pediatrician was never touchy, nor did he ever try to kiss me. This new doctor just wasn't right. I quit seeing Dr. Smith and went to a female doctor with whom I felt much more safe and secure.

Hopefully Dr. Smith's heart has changed. I would hate to

think of other young girls having to go through what I went through. I didn't understand, and I thought it to be normal but later realized nothing he did was normal. The moment a person realizes she was taken advantage of is the moment that person feels violated. I was young and naïve, but with that being said, I know none of it was my fault. For a long time, I blamed myself for going to him and for being so dumb as to think it was okay, but I refuse to let that one person hold me back from moving forward.

During my life I have had many close calls—from getting mononucleosis that almost killed me to major allergic reactions that landed me in the hospital, as well as nearly bleeding out from a tonsillectomy and living through a doctor's inappropriate behavior. But through it all God has been with me, He never left me, nor has He forsaken me.

> "Be strong and of good courage, do not fear nor be afraid of them; for the Lord your God, He is the One who goes with you. He will not leave you nor forsake you."
> (Deuteronomy 31:6)

> "Assuredly, I say to you, whoever does not receive the kingdom of God as a little child will by no means enter it." (Luke 18:17)

It's easy to judge others for their actions, but we as Christians are to have faith like a child trusting God. I lived my life always trusting God; even when I was backsliding, I still believed fully that God was always there for me. He is the One True King.

As I was growing up, my heart was always true. However, it's hard not to allow ourselves to fret over others' wrong doings, but if we walk in faith, through God anything is possible. I do admit that I made many mistakes, and I still make plenty of mistakes. The difference between my mistakes when I was young compared to the mistakes I make now is that I allow growth from every decision, mistake, or correction that happens in my life now. I make sure that not one thing is wasted.

> The discretion of a man makes him slow to anger, And his glory is to overlook a transgression. (Proverbs 19:11)

We are to let go of the things that try to hold us back, for those things are not of God, but yet they come from a deep darkness that will pull us into an abyss if we don't let go.

> [13] Brethren, I do not count myself to have apprehended; but one thing I do, forgetting those things which are behind and reaching forward to those things which are ahead, [14] I press toward the goal for the prize of the upward call of God in Christ Jesus. (Philippians 3:13-14)

It would have been easy for me to be angry at Dr. Smith, to take offense, but when we have faith like a child, we trust that God will take care of those who do wrong in His sight. I'm not saying I shouldn't have reported him, because I should have. I am saying that it is not our job to take revenge, nor should we allow ourselves to harbor a heart full of anger.

> Beloved, do not avenge yourselves, but rather give place to wrath; for it is written, "Vengeance is Mine, I will repay," says the Lord. (Romans 12:19)

Chapter Five

My Fake Fiancé

"You are the salt of the earth;
but if the salt loses its flavor, how shall it be seasoned?
It is then good for nothing
but to be thrown out and trampled underfoot by men."
Matthew 5:13

When we are called in our lives to fulfill God's will, plan, and purpose, we are to do just that, or like the verse says, it is good for nothing. I went through some years in my life where I stepped out of God's will and into my own. Through the stepping out, I was brought to my knees.

I was going to college full-time and also working. I had decided to turn down my scholarship offers in order to stay in the state with my mom. It was her request; if I were to stay, she would pay for my college and help me with anything I needed. I am actually glad I took her offer because it gave me more time with her before God called her home.

Crazy Me

I was nineteen at the time, and I had just started a new job waiting tables at an Olive Garden. I actually loved waiting tables because I was good at it and I loved working. I was great with multi-tasking skills, I also learned how to balance well, and I was amazing with the customers. It was a fun job for me, and I made lots of money doing the job.

This job is also where I met my fake fiancé, Caleb. He was tall and well-built. He always had his hair nicely cut, and he seemed a little shy. I don't know why but I liked the fact that he was too scared to come up to me when all the other guys weren't. I could tell he wanted to talk to me, but I wasn't the type at that time to make the first move. Finally, he made his move, and we went out.

He seemed like a good guy, and we really got along well all throughout our relationship. I actually can't think of one time where we fought. We did everything together except for attend school. He couldn't afford college, and he really didn't like the fact that I was going without him, so I chose to dropout that year.

First Threat

We had been dating for a couple of months when my ex, Roberto, who was still stalking me, showed up at our work. When my ex showed up, he wasn't alone. He had about four or five other guys with him, all in suits and all tough-looking Italians. They all sat at Caleb's table. They were cordial, but when they left, they left a note on the table. The note was a death threat. That night we had to be escorted to our cars in fear that someone was going to follow through with that threat. Thankfully, the threat was not acted on.

Catching On

Caleb had some great qualities about him, but I never understood a couple of things about him. It seemed like he always cried. He took offense quite often, and he didn't seem like he was happy. He was also always jealous of those who had more in life. He was very needy, unlike anyone I would usually be interested in, but for some reason at that moment in my life, I was still interested. I guess his neediness really never stood out until we were done with each other. My mom used to say, "Honey, he isn't your type. He is too needy wanting you to do everything for him." My mom wasn't being rude about her statement. She was just used to guys who treated me well, and she really didn't understand why I would date someone who needed so much attention.

Offended

I remember one day when my boyfriend and I were sitting at a traffic light, I said my saying I have said since I was a kid— "Green, green, booger machine." My brother and I made up this little saying when we rode in my mom's green booger machine, and we often recited it at green lights. The moment I said this, I realized I had made a big mistake; Caleb was so offended and upset because he thought I was calling him a booger machine. When I realized what was happening, I started laughing so loud that I couldn't contain myself. I didn't wish to offend him, nor did I mean anything behind the statement, and when I tried to explain that I wasn't referencing him, he didn't listen. I think he had a hard time believing the fact because he did have a lot of boogers, but I would have never called him a name for that; that wasn't my heart. However, he never saw the humor of the past. I still giggle to this day about that; really it's a phrase that has always stuck with me, and to this day, I still say it from time to time when I am riding in the passenger seat!

I should have seen then what I saw years later. We didn't have the same views of success, and our goals in life were a complete opposite. We didn't even share a similar humor! He really didn't have a passion or a vision for the future; he was completely content staying a waiter, when all I could think about was moving forward. Yes, I loved what I did, but I wanted more in life.

Moving

I had finally decided it was time to move out on my own. It was a new season for me in my life. I had accepted a job as a leasing agent at some apartments in North Oklahoma City; this was really a big deal for me! The great news was that I had free rent because I took on the after hour calls at the apartment, meaning if someone was ever locked out, I would be the one to let them into their apartment.

Even with rent paid, it's very hard to pay utilities and food when all you are making is minimum wage. It was hard at first because I grew up getting whatever I wanted or needed, and suddenly I had to watch what I spent. Through it all, I somehow made it work. Sometimes we grow in the hard times—and I sure did!

I was all moved out and out on my own, but Caleb was still stuck in the past. He did not have much drive, and that is okay, but when you have someone who is driven to succeed dating someone who only wants to have fun in life, clashes start to take place. Even still, I thought I was in love. We had been dating for almost a year, and we were now pretty serious to the point that we started looking at rings. I did find a ring I loved but he couldn't afford it, so he asked for me to buy the ring (Yes, I know what you're thinking, and you're right). We both made a rule that I wouldn't wear it until he had paid for the ring and then formally asked for my hand in marriage. He never ended up paying for the ring so after a long while I decided I was going to wear the ring. It was beautiful, and after all, I had paid for this sparkly ring that was just sitting in his truck. I wore the ring, but wasn't engaged, which is why I say, "My Fake Fiancé." Caleb also wanted others to know I was taken, but he never wanted to take the steps in asking formally. I guess I knew deep down we would never get married, but still, I thought I was in love.

Waiting for Marriage

A year went by, and we were still dating. I was twenty-one

and still a virgin because I was taught that you wait until marriage to have physical union with a man, and to this I stayed true, but something that year snapped. It wasn't lust, it wasn't because I really loved him, because I wasn't fully sure (I thought I did, but I still questioned it). It wasn't anything but the fact that I felt like he was checking out mentally and I had never had a guy that I cared about leave me and I wasn't ready for him to go.

The Night

I planned a big dinner at my apartment with everything nice and romantic, including the fireplace blazing and music softly playing. After dinner that night, I gave myself to him. The moment I gave myself to him, I lost something special that he never deserved. After I had opened up to him, I remember lying next to him trying to justify my sin; I kept trying to reason with God so that the guilt wouldn't fall over me. This was my first step away from God.

> [18] Flee sexual immorality. Every sin that a man does is outside the body, but he who commits sexual immorality sins against his own body. [19] Or do you not know that your body is the temple of the Holy Spirit who is in you, whom you have from God, and you are not your own? [20] For you were bought at a price; therefore glorify God in your body and in your spirit, which are God's. (1 Corinthians 6:18-20)

I had never been with anyone, and I had heard stories where it was awful the first time, and yes, it was awful. I also heard stories where girls cried afterwards, but I wasn't built that way; I don't cry too easily. However, Caleb did cry. I didn't understand at first why he was crying because he had been with other girls before; in fact, some had claimed he had gotten them pregnant, but, of course, he denied them all, and only God knows the truth.

I figured it out later that he cried because of guilt. He was already seeing someone else, yet had just taken my virginity. To make matters more painful, he was seeing a friend of mine that I actually helped get hired at the Olive Garden.

Two weeks after that big night, he broke up with me. I guess he felt he owed me a couple of weeks before breaking up since I had just given him my virginity; I don't know. I do know he was mentally gone, and the moment I noticed he was checking out, I should have just let him go. But through it all, I did end up reaping what I sowed.

The day we broke up I was at my best friend's dorm. Caleb told me over the phone that he was done. I was crushed. I remember yelling at him, being broken, telling him that I gave him everything. I even knew at that moment that I was probably pregnant. The moment we hung up, I went to my best friend's restroom just physically sick. How could I have given him something he didn't deserve? Later I thought about it and realized that when we step into sin, we are stepping into heartache and disappointment.

A week went by and I was extremely stressed and depressed. Caleb had called a few times, but I didn't want to talk. After a few calls from him, I finally answered the phone, and that is when he told me that he had made a huge mistake and that he was asking me back. He asked if I would go out with him that night, and I did.

We went to dinner at another Olive Garden to talk where we didn't know anybody. We were back together but nothing felt right. Dinner that night was a changing point for me. Where I once felt sadness and despair for him, that night turned to disgust. I don't know what did it for me—if it was the fact that I told him I thought I was pregnant and he told me that we would take care of it if I was, or if God opened my eyes to see him for who he really was.

He had lost me. Caleb called me after he dropped me off at my mom's house, which was where I left my car. When he called, he started with the sentence, "I'm not sure." That was it. It was all I needed. I was completely done, and I was okay with never being with him ever again. Before he could say another word, I stopped him and gave him a little talk, one that was about thirty minutes long. When I was done talking, he was crying, and the conversation was over, as were we.

One thing I did tell him was that if I happened to be pregnant, I would rather be a single mother then to be a parent with him. I knew that if I was pregnant I could be a great strong single mom; after all, I was raised by the best.

Out of our relationship, many hurts took place, and they were not all his fault because I subjected myself to them as well. But because of him, for a long time I never let a guy show his feelings in front of me. I couldn't stand seeing a guy cry, and if he did cry, he lost all respect from me. Because of Caleb, I went through many years of being cold-hearted. And because of that cold heart, God had to break me, and break me He would.

Now that I look back on my ex and our relationship, I wish I would have known then that he really needed help. I feel bad for him and now all I can do is pray for him.

Remember: A tender heart goes a long way. Before my ex, I had a tender heart, but because of him, I grew a little colder and I became a little bit broken. I was not the same person I was prior to my relationship with Caleb; part of my light had gone out. Of course, when God got ahold of me, a lot of things changed.

> Finally, all of you be of one mind, having compassion for one another; love as brothers, be tenderhearted, be courteous;
> (1 Peter 3:8)

Chapter Six
No, God!

For I know the thoughts that I think toward you,
says the Lord, thoughts of peace and not of evil,
to give you a future and a hope.
Jeremiah 29:11

A month after giving myself to Caleb, I was sick, sick, sick, and praying: *No, God, I can't be pregnant.* I didn't want to be pregnant, and I felt like if I was, it would embarrass my mom and bring shame to my name. Being pregnant without being married was against everything I was ever raised to be.

The continued sickness didn't stop, so I decided to take a pregnancy test. It came back negative. I took a couple more about two weeks later, and both of those tests came back negative as well. I finally went to the doctor because I couldn't get over being sick. I had no insurance and was living off of minimum wage, so I barely had enough money to pay bills let alone go to a doctor, but I knew I needed to go because I wasn't getting any better. When I got to the doctor's office, they confirmed in a blood test what I already knew. I was pregnant. Now, I had the hardest job ever; I had to tell my mom.

I went to see my mom at her house to break the news. I remember that night so vividly. She was sitting in her favorite chair while I paced back and forth in the living room. For some reason I think better when I pace. I didn't know how I was going to break the news to my mom that night, but I needed to tell her. While I was pacing, she knew something was wrong, so she kept asking me, "What is wrong?"

All I could say in return was "You don't want to know."

She finally said in a joking manner because she really didn't believe it would be possible, "You're not pregnant, are you?"

There was no beating around the bush. I confessed, "Yes, Mom, I am."

I have never seen my mom so disappointed in me as she was that night. She was broken, and so was I. I didn't know how I was going to raise a baby, but I knew I was going to make it happen.

While I was on a roll, I went ahead and called Caleb to let him know as well. He didn't really have much to say. When I told him I needed help with doctor's bills, he said he would pay half the bills, but I only received one check from him for eleven dollars. No matter what, it was okay; God took care of us, and I forgave Caleb. I found out later in life that

---

he had become a police officer and actually married the girl that was my friend from our old job. I do wish them the best in life. I really hope they are blessed and that in everything they found peace in God.

Life Decision

When I found out I was pregnant, I had many people ask me if I thought about having an abortion, and this is what I told them: *I made the decision to sleep with someone outside of marriage; I made the decision not to use protection. This baby did nothing wrong, so why punish him by taking his life? Only murderers get the death penalty and I will not give my child the death penalty. Yes, God is the judge, but I am the juror and I made the decision.*

As a result, I was pregnant, sick, living on my own, and without insurance. Even with everything feeling like it was all crashing down, I still lived my life. I worked out about four times a week if not more, and during this time, I was mentally preparing myself to be a single mom.

At four months pregnant, I was working out at a gym where nobody there knew I was pregnant. I had a flat stomach because I was tiny at that time and this was my first pregnancy so I wasn't showing yet. While I was working out at this new gym, I befriended a trainer there. However, when I finally started showing, this new friend went and told everyone at the gym that I was having his baby. I didn't understand how someone I barely knew, was never with, and didn't plan on being with, could go and try to take claim over me and my baby. I was so upset that I quit going to work out at that gym. I realized that no matter what, even being pregnant, I had to be careful of those who would try to slither their way into my life. Just because I was pregnant and single didn't mean I was weak and needed a man to fill a void that wasn't there. I was actually okay with being single.

Getting Help

I was now in a position that I had never been in before. I needed help. This was when I found out about state-provided assistance that was offered to women who were pregnant and without options. I was given food, and my doctor bills were paid for, but I didn't want to have to rely on someone or a system to provide for me, so I re-evaluated my life and where I was, which led me to decide that I needed to make a change. I decided that my job wasn't going to do for a single mother so I needed a better paying one, and I needed to move back in with my mom until I could get back on my feet. She was the support I needed spiritually, physically, and mentally, and thankfully she was there for me even if she was disappointed. She still loved me through it all.

Home Again

Life was good being back home with my mom. I was going to doctors and was at peace being at my mom's house, which was my true home. At the same time, I was blessed with an amazing job that paid really well, and it had insurance! Thank you, God! After getting this amazing job, I went ahead and called the place that approved for me to get help. I told them that I wasn't in need of their assistance anymore because I now had a better paying job and insurance. I was then informed that I was already approved to go ahead and keep what they were giving me as backup. I felt bad because I didn't want to abuse what was given once as a blessing, but I did as the worker told me and thank the Lord I did.

Baby Joys

At sixteen weeks pregnant, I went to the hospital to see if I was having a boy or a girl—and I was so happy to learn that my baby was a boy. I couldn't have been more excited, so my mom and I started to plan for his arrival. We bought outfits, a crib, and decorated his room. We were set and ready.

During this time, my first ex, Roberto, tried to come back into my life. He offered to raise the baby as his own. Another friend of mine that went to my church made an offer to take me as his wife and raise my baby as his own as well. I didn't have feelings for either man, and I was actually very shocked about the offer from my friend. I looked at the situation like this—it didn't matter if they thought they were in love with me or if I was single, you don't marry for those reasons. And I was still okay being single. I was very happy knowing I was about to be a mommy. I wasn't even in the mindset of thinking about a man. I was only thinking about my little boy who would be here soon.

Time was coming along and my baby needed a name! I

am big on names; I believe a name can be a blessing or a curse. When you speak a name, you are speaking over the person, so I prayed hard to see what God would want me to name my son. While praying when I was in bed one night, God showed me what his name would be: *Abiah,* meaning "the LORD is my Father." My mom was not too keen on the name Abiah; in fact, she begged for me to change it to something else. I just kept on praying, and I felt at peace. God said, "Don't worry, she will love the name, and this is what his name is to be." What better name than claiming God as our Father? I felt very connected to my son, of course. We both had an amazing Father in heaven, and that was a seed that we both shared together.

News

Time was getting close, and it was time for the baby shower. I love presents! My mom and others planned a couple of baby showers, and I couldn't wait to go see what all my son was going to get. However, before we ever went to the first baby shower, I found out some of the worst news a mother could ever find out about her baby.

I was thirty-two weeks pregnant and in my doctor's office for a regular office visit when it happened. The ultrasound technologist kept looking at Abiah, and she had this look, a dreaded look as if something was wrong. She then said she would be back and left the room. I knew at that moment something was not right, and I was correct on that assumption. When the technologist came back, she wasn't alone; she had my doctor with her. When my doctor came into the room, he had a serious look on his face, but he went straight to checking my baby, not saying a word yet. As he was checking, he had that same look the tech had. I knew something was wrong, but nothing could prepare me for what I was about to hear. The doctor gently said, "Honey, your son doesn't have a fully developed heart."

What was I hearing? Could this be true? No, God, this can't be true! The doctor then went on to say that he had only seen this condition before in books; my son was the first he had ever seen in real life. After speaking with us, he sent us on to a specialist, who confirmed the condition, and we knew we needed to start planning to get my son help.

Hypoplastic Left Heart Syndrome

My son was diagnosed with Hypoplastic Left Heart Syndrome. What this meant was that his left ventricle of his heart wasn't fully developed. (Babies with Hypoplastic Left Heart Syndrome are called blue babies because they are born with blue hands and feet.) I was told that not many babies had been diagnosed with this yet, so it was something many doctors hadn't seen. Only recently they have started realizing this was also one of the causes of many SIDS cases. It was explained to me that babies would have this defect, and many would go undetected. The babies with this defect would be sent home, and then they would pass away within days. The news was horrible, but I kept telling myself that we were blessed that we caught it before he was born, so we could plan for him to get help once he arrived. I was trying to find some positive out of the horrible news we were given.

Specialist after Specialist

I was seeing a specialist for my pregnancy as well as heart surgeons and heart specialist. What were the odds? What could I do? The odds didn't look good, but I had two options: a full heart transplant or a three-surgery process, which meant his first surgery would be within days of birth. His chances of living through the first surgery at that time were low and the odds of him living past twenty-four to forty-eight hours after the surgery were even lower. The first twenty-four to forty-eight hours were the most critical.

If we decided to do the heart transplant, first there was a chance he wouldn't even get a heart and would pass away while waiting, or he could get the heart and then his body could reject it. Our chances of him living was higher with the three-step process, so after a lot of prayer and talking with my mom, we decided the best option would be the three-surgery process.

After deciding on the surgery, we then decided what doctor would be best to do the job. God provided us with the best in the nation. He was from South Africa, extremely good at his job, and he really cared about his patients. The surgeon's plan: the day Abiah was born, we would give him medicine to trick his body into thinking he was still in the womb. This medicine would trick his body so the heart flap would stay open so he could get strong and ready for surgery. Once he was strong enough, we would go into surgery, probably within 10 days of birth.

Baby Shower

All the way to the baby shower, I was in deep thought. I didn't know if my son was going to live, and I kept thinking about opening presents when I didn't know if they would be used or not. The thought was killing me within. I kept thinking about how I would be able to live if he died, and if he did die, what was I going to do?

At this time, I hadn't told but a handful of people about my son and his heart because I didn't want people to speak negatively or to speak words of death.

> Death and life are in the power of the tongue,
> And those who love it will eat its fruit.
> (Proverbs 18:21)

I wanted only those who would pray for him to know. Going to the baby shower, it became apparent something was wrong. I tried to act like everything was great—I enjoyed every kick and every move my son made. I held on to the feeling of him being alive because I refused to let that moment be taken away, the moment of knowing he was still okay, still alive.

The hardest part was the fact that I had some people make fun of me at the shower for being so stuck on the "watch this" or "look at him move." Those who laughed had no clue what was going on inside and how my heart was breaking every moment. Those who laughed had never had a baby before that moment, nor had they been in a position of losing a child. They had no clue about the hurt, the pain of not knowing what was going to happen to their child. They didn't know the feelings of trying to stay positive when the outcome looked bad on the outside. They had never gone through anything like knowing this time could be the only time I had with my child—I was trying to take in every minute I could.

The fear of knowing there was nothing I as a mother could do but just pray; the fear of knowing this child I was carrying might not come home with me from the hospital—those are the worst feelings a mother could ever have, feelings of helplessness, brokenness, and complete heartache.

Chapter Seven
Little Abiah

¹³ For You formed my inward parts;
You covered me in my mother's womb.
¹⁴ I will praise You,
for I am fearfully and wonderfully made;
Marvelous are Your works,
And that my soul knows very well.
¹⁵ My frame was not hidden from You,
When I was made in secret,
And skillfully wrought in the lowest parts of the earth.
¹⁶ Your eyes saw my substance, being yet unformed.
And in Your book they all were written,
The days fashioned for me,
When as yet there were none of them.
Psalm 139:13-16

It was time to deliver my precious gift. I was being induced so the doctors could be ready. Everything was planned.

My specialist was in the room, along with twenty other doctors and nurses who all wanted to see my son, since seeing a baby with this defect was rare at this time. Because they wanted my son close to the children's hospital, I had to have him in the connecting hospital, not my hospital of choice, but we made changes to make sure he was going to be taken care of properly.

I had about forty family members at the hospital the day he was born, and after eighteen hours of labor, he was finally here—July 15, 1999, at 7:38 p.m. He was immediately rushed out the door on his way to the Neonatal Intensive Care Unit (NICU). I had only seconds to lay eyes on my precious baby before they took off with him, but I could see that he was a perfect creation of God—6 lbs, 7 oz, and 19 ¼ inches long.

NICU

I walked in to the NICU to see him for the first time, and I thought, "So this is what you look like" as I watched him suck on his hand and wrist. Oh how I loved the feeling of knowing he was mine! I was overwhelmed with love for my precious son.

By the time I got to see Abiah, he already had IVs and tubes hooked up to him. He was still perfect in every way. His voice was deep, his fingers were long, and his feet were big with long toes. He was beautiful and smart. Every time I would come in the room, he would stop crying because he knew his mommy was there, way before I even said a word. He knew his mommy.

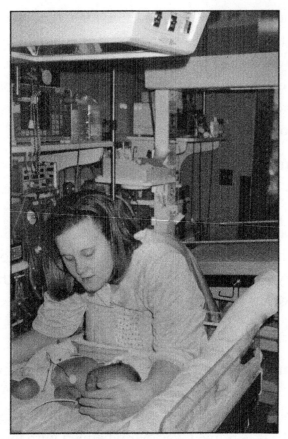

The day of Abiah's birth, July 15, 1999

My Baby

He didn't like being messed with, so he learned very early to play possum when the nurses came around. He knew that if he pretended to be asleep, they would leave him alone! When I would stand next to him, he would hold my finger, and what a great grip he had. He would hold me as long as I would stand by him.

On July 19, the day before surgery, they said he had jaundice, so they put him under the lights. Poor boy, I felt so sorry for him. He wanted so badly for his eyes to be uncovered. His little feet were so bruised from being stuck repeatedly for blood work. I wanted to trade places with him, if only if I could. That day, the surgeon came in and told me to be careful touching him because if I were to pull his main line out, it would kill him. He also explained that the surgery the next day would be very, very dangerous. The surgery was so delicate that the possibility existed that Abiah could have a stroke in the middle of it all. Since it was open heart surgery, there were also many more risks. The surgeon could not even promise me that my son would make it through surgery. As the tears ran down my face, reality hit that this could be my last day to see him alive. The surgeon ended the conversation by reassuring me, "I will be praying for your son, and I will do the best I can for him."

He was born on July 15, and five short days later, on the 20th, he went into full reconstructive heart surgery. I would have done anything for him to not to have to go through all of the surgery and procedures, but in Abiah's best interests and chances for survival, I allowed it all.

The Day of Surgery
The morning of the surgery, after only getting an hour or so of sleep, I went into Abiah's room around 5:15 a.m. just to hold my baby boy. As I held him close, all the longing and wanting to hold him just came all out. I held and rocked him

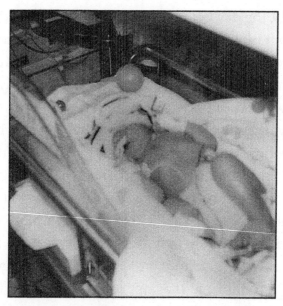

The day before his surgery, July 19, 1999.

gently as I talked to him. He just loved being in my arms and laid there so gently. I held him until they were ready to take him to surgery around 7:00 a.m. Oh, if I knew then what I know now, I would have died before leaving him in that room. He was sleeping so peacefully; he looked so beautiful. They took him as I cried and told him I loved him.

No parent should ever have to go through the pain of walking next to their child as they are rolled in a bed, down a hall, into surgery. The fear of not knowing if he would make it out alive is what kept me sick to my stomach and in constant prayer. We had many visitors there for him, wanting to see him and meet me, but during this time I didn't care about anything but my son and his endurance through this

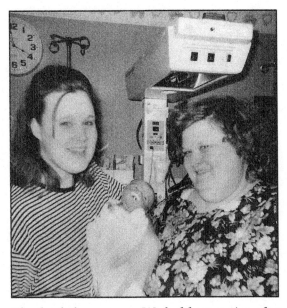

The day before surgery. We had been crying after speaking with the doctors, and I was still very swollen from giving birth. It felt unnatural to smile, but we were trying to be positive.

surgery. My desire was to take him home, to be his mommy ,and to take care of him. I loved him more than life itself, and I still love him.

As I walked my son down the hall in his bed, I myself was still recovering from a hard labor and delivery just days before, but my thoughts were on nothing but taking in every moment, every look, every inch of who he was. His color, his beautiful face, his lips, eyes, hair, arms, legs, fingers and toes—I couldn't get enough of how beautiful and perfect he was; nothing about him looked like anything was wrong.

While we were in the waiting room, a pastor from a large

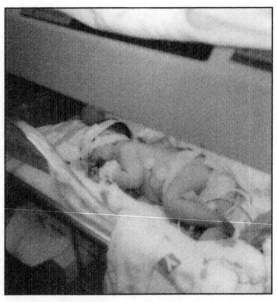

The day before surgery. His foot was bruised from all of the pricking they did for tests.

church I had never even heard of showed up and said he had heard of my son, so he came down to the hospital to give me support and to let me know that the people in his church were praying for my son. Churches all around the world were praying for him. The support and love of God's people was incredible; despite my worries and tortuous waiting, I knew my son was in the Lord's hands.

Surgery was supposed to take six to eight hours, but after only five-and-a-half hours, he was out. The doctor came and gave the report: everything went amazingly—in fact, better than expected. However, it was explained that the forty-eight hours following surgery were the most critical. If he lived through the next forty-eight hours, then he would be doing great, and we would be past the worst part of this three-surgery process.

As I waited in the hallway for permission to see my son, I saw a family whose daughter-in-law had had twins. One of the babies was born with the same defect Abiah had, but it went unnoticed, and that baby was sent home without any help. As I sat there watching that family mourn, it broke me to see their hurt, but I knew then that God had a reason we caught Abiah's early.

Post-Surgery

I wanted to see my baby, and all I could do was sit there and wait until I was given permission to go back and see him. When I was finally given permission to see Abiah, I was told by the doctor that he wouldn't look like himself; that it was going to be hard to see him like this, but to try to stay strong for him because he could feel his mommy and not to let him feel that fear or stress. I was also told that tubes and tape would be all over him.

No matter the warnings or speech, nothing could prepare me for what I walked into. I entered my son's room at the end of the hall, the largest room on the floor. He had multiple machines hooked up to him and all around him. He had tubes coming out of his chest, and his body was completely taped and wrapped up. He was swollen and, of course, not coherent. Tears came down my face nonstop for hours. I tried to sing and pray over him, but the sight of the condition he was in was breaking me to the point of being completely gone. No words can describe seeing any baby in this condition, and when it's your own baby, it was like losing all feeling and strength in my body. My heart hurt so bad; at times I thought I was dying, and many times I didn't care if I did die. No words. Nothing can describe how awful this was, and the worst part was that I could do nothing to help him. That day, I will never forget.

Life at the Hospital

I was a young mother, but I wasn't leaving. I was even told by many nurses there that they had never seen such a young parent there as much as I was. Day and night I stayed in Abiah's room. When I did leave his room, I went into the waiting room to sleep on the floor. After a few days of sleeping out in the waiting room, the hospital ended up giving me a room there to sleep in. We had to pay for it each day like a hotel room, but the church paid the fees for us. Thank You, Lord.

Soon I was able to go see him anytime and as much as I wanted, so having a place to take a nap when needed was so appreciated. It was wonderful to be able to spend as much time with him as possible, and yet I had to take naps, even if it was for only a few hours at a time. Thanks to good friends who took care of getting my clothes from home occasionally, I only actually left the hospital one time for a couple of hours, a brief hiatus that I later came to regret.

During our stay, a baby in the room next to ours never had visitors. My heart broke for that little baby. I even wanted to go in there and hold him, but at that time they didn't allow visitors to do such a thing. I was told that the nurses would go in there and take turns holding him. I couldn't understand how a parent could have a child who was sick and never be there to be with the child. I couldn't understand how someone could be away in that situation. Many days during this time of my life were heartbreaking. I witnessed children passing during that stay, and I cried a lot for other families and for those babies, but mostly during this time I cried to God for a miracle.

My son was past the worst part of the surgery, and he was recovering well. He was going to be okay! His swelling was all gone, and he looked healthy once again. He was perfect in every way.

The entire hospital stay, my mom stayed with me. I thank the Lord for my mom; she was so amazing. I thank God He allowed her to be there during this time in my life.

Friends, family, and church members were so supportive of us, and we had tons of visitors daily. People who didn't even know us flew in to meet me, as they had heard about my son and wanted to give me support. I had other mothers who had children with the same defect come to visit with me. One mother even brought her son along to show me that my child could be just as normal as any other. This child had gone through the surgeries my son was going to go through in life. This little boy was so cute; when he stood before me, he lifted his shirt to show me his scar. It was nice having many around who supported us.

The church was praying for my son, and many other churches as well. Word went across the world—we even had letters from people we had never met letting us know they were praying.

My Son's Song

Every day I played "Draw Me Close" over and over in Abiah's room to the point that my son's doctor thought I was crazy, I am sure. I don't know why this song was his song in particular, but all I knew was that it touched my heart every time it played.

"Draw Me Close"

Songwriter: Kelly Robert Carpenter
©1994 Mercy/Vineyard Publishing
CCLI#1459484

Draw me close to You
Never let me go
I lay it all down again
To hear You say that I'm Your friend

You are my desire
And no one else will do
'Cause nothing else can take Your place
To feel the warmth of Your embrace

Help me find a way
Bring me back to You

You're all I want

You're all I've ever needed
You're all I want
Help me know You are near

Abiah

During our stay at the hospital, I heard that there was a huge discussion between the nurses. They were questioning my son's name, *Abiah*. One nurse reportedly said, "Who would ever do that to their child?" While the other nurse replied, "You have no idea what she has gone through and you have no right to say anything. If you knew the story, you would never question that name. That name is perfect." His name is perfect. *Abiah, The LORD is my Father.* My mom came to terms with it, like God told me she would, shortly after we found out about his heart defect. "You couldn't have picked a better name" is what she told me; however, I didn't pick the name—the Father gave it to me. Abiah was meant to be; he had a purpose, and still does. God knew him before he was ever born.

> "Before I formed you in the womb I knew you;
> Before you were born I sanctified you; I ordained you a prophet to the nations."
> (Jeremiah 1:5)

Yes, Father

In early August, I was sitting in a chair next to him, praying like I always did. During that prayer God asked me, "Do you mind if I take him early?"

Being a mother, I never thought, nor would I allow myself to think, about that question as meaning death, so I debated in my head what God could be meaning. I changed the question around in my head and considered if God was asking if I would let him "take him early", perhaps meaning he would go into mission work at a young age. I even thought about the young ages of eleven and twelve. I thought about how I would feel if my son had to leave to go across the world. Would I let him go?

"Yes, Father," was my answer. Who was I to question God? If He needed to take Abiah to do His work early, then at least he would be fulfilling his God-called purpose. Of this I wasn't comfortable, but I was at least at peace.

A couple of days later God came down and took my son to be with Him in heaven. I often think about what my life would have turned out to be like if I would have said NO to God. Abiah would be alive, but would his life be a good life? Would he enjoy life and health? On July 15, 2015, he would have been sixteen years old—old enough to drive. Wow, thinking about training him to drive is unfathomable. I am crying just thinking about what it would be like.

Before He Went Home

My son was doing amazingly well before he passed. I was even told he would be going to the other floor, and they were preparing to send him home within the next week. I was so excited I could hardly stand it. I kept thinking about how he was going to be home, in my arms, with me. His room was ready and waiting for him, and I was so ready to be his mommy, to take care of him, to hold him, and to tell him how much I loved him every chance I got. I loved him so much that I was beside myself.

The Day I Lost My Heart

Monday morning, August 9, I went into my son's room to find a different nurse than any of his normal nurses. My son had nurses who loved him; I actually grew great relationships with many of them. But this morning was different. The nurse that day, I had never seen before. I was told from some of the other nurses that the hospital was so busy they had to pull the regular nurses to help other children who were in bad shape, and that because my son was doing so well, they knew he would be okay with the nurse from the other department who was filling in.

That was also the day that the resident accidently overdosed my son, and because the new nurse wasn't one of his regular nurses, she didn't catch the error, nor did she know to question the error.

That day I started noticing that my son was starting to swell back up, and not only that, he also had red patches all over his body. When I called it to the attention of one of my son's regular nurses, she said, "I wonder if it's what the resident did?" That statement scared me, so I started asking questions. It was then I discovered the resident's mistake—he had accidentally given Abiah too much of the medication he was on. I called my son's heart surgeon and requested that he come see Abiah immediately. When the surgeon got to my son's room to check on him, he was confused as to why my son's blood acids had shot up. I asked him if it could be what the resident had done. In response, he looked at me in complete confusion and said, "What did he do?" After I told him the limited information I knew, I could tell it was bad.

The surgeon immediately started calling in a ton of specialists. I had no clue at that time what was going on or why he was calling in all of the help. While he was in the room, I sat outside in the hallway in complete confusion as to what he was so worried about. I had no clue at that time what this medicine could do to Abiah, only that he had been given more instead of less. It was nighttime, and as I sat there waiting for the surgeon to come out, I had no clue what was about to happen.

When the surgeon finally emerged to speak with me the next morning, he explained that he was going to be bringing in yet another specialist to look at my son. I was running on no sleep, just waiting for the specialist, praying for a miracle. An endless stream of doctors, specialists, and hospital staff, including the surgeon, had been going in and out of Abiah's room all night.

Finally, they were done with their examinations and the time arrived to hear their determinations; but as the heart surgeon walked out, he had a look on his face that I tried to ignore. He came up to me and more fully explained what had happened to Abiah. Hyperal is a nutritional supplementation they were giving him through the IV. The surgeon said that too much of Hyperal would crystallize the kidneys, and then from there the blood acids in the body shoot up. A Hyperal overdose is like being eaten from the inside out. He continued to say that there was nothing that they could do—my son was not going to make it. The moment those words left his mouth was the moment my legs gave out and I hit the ground. My son was going to die.

From what I was told later, the resident had been up for three days straight. A couple of nurses informed me that the resident wrote *increase by double* on his Hyperal orders instead of *decrease by double*. The simple little mistake of *in-* instead of *de-* took my son's life. My son had to die over someone being tired.

Despite my intense grief, I truly believed God was going to give us a miracle. I just knew God was going to heal my son. I was fully convinced that my little boy was going to go home with me—I could envision us at home together in his room, me caring for him as he grew up. I just knew I was going to get to be a mom. I loved my son! Why would God take Abiah from me, a mom who loved her child and would die for him? So many parents out there hurt their children and don't even want their children! But, oh, God, I loved my son! Why would You take my child away? This was something that went through my head over and over for years.

The day my son passed we had a ton of family and friends who loved us there at the hospital. I was even told by a sweet lady that God was there and that He personally was going to take my son home. All of our guests were in his room that day. Before they had only allowed up to two guests at a time, but anytime a child was dying they always allowed however many the family wanted present. I had seen it happen on other occasions where the family and friends would go into the room and grieve together. I just never dreamed it would happen to me. I can't even remember who all was present, other than my mom and many others filling the room. My mind wasn't on anything or anyone but my son.

On his last day, I was finally allowed to hold him for the first time since his surgery. He was still hooked up to every-thing, but he was slowly leaving. I could hear his heart beating on the monitor and that gave me hope. As I held him the doctor said he was in a lot of pain, that he couldn't tell us, but he needed something for the pain. I cried, holding him close in my arms. As his heart was still beating, I kept telling him I was sorry. Over and over I cried, "I'm sorry, I'm sorry, I'm sorry!" I cried this to the point that those were the only words I remember telling him as I held him. I know we are told in mourning that it's not our fault, but no matter how much someone tells you that it's not your fault, being the parent you always feel you could have done something differently to change the outcome. *I'm sorry you had the heart defect—was it something I ate? Something I did? What did I do to cause this?* As I held my sweet little Abiah, I begged that my heart could beat for his, but it was too late. His heart was slowly stopping to the point of no more. I held my son in my arms as his heart took its last beats. Tuesday, August 10, 1999, was the day I lost my son, lost my faith, and lost my heart. I was completely broken.

As the people left the room, I gave my son his last sponge bath, and I changed him. By this time, a few nurses were in the room with me and the resident who had made the mistake was at the entrance of the room, with tears in his eyes. He said he was very sorry, but I couldn't listen to him. I had become deaf to everything going on around me. It was like life was happening, but I wasn't there.

My Son's Obituary

COBB, Christian Abiah (*God is My Father*), son of Christina Cobb, born July 15, 1999, went to be with his Father, August 10, 1999. Although his entire life was spent in the hospital, he was a fighter and had a will to live for his Mommy and Grandma, Joyce Cobb, both of whom stayed with him during his short life. He took a part of their hearts with him. He will be greatly missed by numerous loved ones. Mommy loves you, Christian, and will never forget you.

Chapter Eight

Broken

"My spirit is broken,
My days are extinguished,
The grave is ready for me."
Job 17:1

When Abiah was gone, I sat alone in his room at home with his crib, his clothes, and all the décor up on the walls. I'm not sure how long I sat there, but I know it was hours, maybe days. For a long time, I didn't go anywhere but to see him at the funeral home and then back home. I didn't shower, I didn't talk to anyone, and I was completely gone.

In my pain, I was often asking God, "Why?" Like Job, I knew I had no right to question God, but my hurt ran so deep. *Lord, why did my son have to hurt, why?* I wished as any mother who loses a child that I could just hold Abiah and show him my love. I wished I could play with him and show him this world could be a beautiful place, that there was more to it than the hospital and doctors and nurses and surgery and pain. I wished so many things could have been changed, but no matter what, I would never have changed how deep my love was for my baby. I loved you then, Christian Abiah, and I still do.

Before Abiah's funeral day was upon us, I was told it would be best to call my ex and let him know that his son had passed. I didn't want to call him because he never wanted anything to do with my son. I had even lost all respect for his mother, who had tried to talk me into having an abortion when I first found out I was pregnant. At the time, my response to her suggestion was that I would never do that to my child and that God had a plan and purpose for him. I explained that I would take care of him, and I didn't need her or her son's help. Caleb had not shown any interest in my pregnancy or the baby, so at Abiah's passing, I was very reluctant to inform them of this great sadness.

My instincts turned out to be correct, but I made the phone call anyway. I called Caleb and explained that Abiah had passed away and that he could go see him at the funeral home. His response was "I already have plans." I don't recall saying anything after that, but his "plans" kept him from ever seeing the precious gift God gave us for a short moment in time. In all actuality, Abiah's true father was in heaven taking care of him all along.

The Day of the Funeral

We had a burial service at the graveside. We were very bless-

I am holding the casket on my lap after the service was over. My mom was trying to convince me to go, but I just couldn't leave Abiah.

ed by the funeral home and the cemetery, which donated a casket and the grave, as well as provided Abiah's services for us for free. All we had to pay for was the opening and closing of his grave. In everything and with all those who supported us during this time, many donated money to help with cost. With the donated money, we paid for the opening and closing of his grave.

The outpouring of visitors to Abiah's service was huge. Every nurse that had taken care of my son attended. How nurses were able to come and be away from the hospital, I don't know, but there were a lot. So many people attended that I remember the funeral director saying they had never seen so many people at a baby's funeral. I was told people flew in to support us, including a general in the army who had written my son a letter prior to his passing. So many people filled that place, and I still can't remember anything but being surrounded by many faceless people covering the cemetery grounds, and my picking up the tiny casket and just holding it. I can't remember anything that was said, I don't think I talked to anyone there, and I have no clue about the rest of that day.

My Son's Headstone

My brother and I didn't want a headstone that was like others. We wanted something unique and different, so he helped me by writing the perfect thing for my son's headstone: *My heart will always beat for yours. I love you, Sugar Bear.* It took a long time to find a place that would use my son's handprint, but I found someone, and then I signed it, *Mommy.*

We have since seen the same headstone company copy our design by using what we wrote for other graves, changing the nickname, but even using *my son's handprint and my own signature.* Wow—it took a lot of prayer to get past that. At first it upset me seeing the company reusing our headstone for other babies, but after I had time to think about it (years later), I realized that we have blessed others. Those who have gone through the worst loss in the world now had somewhere to visit with more than just a headstone. It has a print

Abiah's headstone today

of my son on it, along with my signature. With love my heart goes out to all those who have lost a child.

Panic Attacks

After my son's death, I started having major panic attacks. I had never had one before in my life, but all of a sudden I started having them quite often. Every time I would try to go somewhere, I would freak out and go into a rocking trance, trying to calm myself. I thought I was going crazy, and I probably was.

I even had one attack land me in the hospital. A month after Abiah's death, my mom got some of the family together to persuade me to leave the house. They were taking me to my favorite restaurant, which was Outback Steakhouse. Leaving the house was one of the hardest things for me to do. When we got to the restaurant, I lost it. My body started going into convulsions, like the shakes, but I couldn't stop it, I couldn't breathe, and I started crying to the point that they rushed me to the hospital. When I got to the hospital, the nurse asked my mom if I had been through anything traumatic recently and my mom responded that I had just lost my infant son. The nurse told me that he went through the same thing a year prior when he lost his son. He also explained to me that what I was going through was shock—my body was in shock, something I found out to be very normal for parents who have lost a child.

No matter how normal the hospital said the shock was, I thought I was going crazy. They drugged me up that night and that was the start of my next few years of being on high doses of anti-depressants and anxiety meds.

The medication dulled a lot of the pain, but it did not stop the panic attacks. They were so awful that I thought I was dying. One time we were leaving to go to Texas, and I tried to get my mom to turn the car around multiple times to take me home. But my mom and brother were determined to get me out of the house.

The panic attacks got worse, so the anti-depressants got stronger in doses. Before being on the really high doses of anti-depressants, I remember my mom holding me like a child and rocking as she prayed over me, speaking in tongues. During this time, I now believe I could have been in full possession. I would have never admitted this before because I never believed it until recently. But, I remember I could hear things coming for me, the attack was so strong. I could hear breathing, like the demons were standing next to me as I would go to bed. One night I even heard someone walking on our roof, and when I went into the house, it followed. This was when my mom really started getting concerned. I didn't know then, but I know now, that I was the meat for the hungry vulture—the prince of the air. When we are at our weakest, it is then the devil tries to attack us. I was the weakest, easiest prey, and I was letting myself wallow in this victimization.

> Be sober, be vigilant; because your adversary
> the devil walks about like a roaring lion, seek-
> ing whom he may devour. (1 Peter 5:8)

The Choice to Live

After a long time of this miserable life--not leaving the house but to go to the cemetery and being under constant attack--I was still having many panic attacks. My Uncle Tony whom I love and respect very much came up to me and said, "Christina, you can either let this make you, or you can let this break you. It's your choice."

Now many people had inadvertently upset me before in conversation, saying things like "I understand", "Stay strong", and "Give your troubles to God." Well, no, you don't understand—if you haven't lost a child, you have no right to say you understand. I couldn't stay strong, and I was under such attack that I wasn't paying much attention to God—at least, not enough to entrust Him with my greatest troubles.

When my uncle spoke these words to me, instead of getting upset, I took them to heart. He had every right to speak these words to me. He himself had lost a son (my cousin) many years prior to my loss. He wasn't speaking blindly, or in slogans—he was speaking as someone who knew my pain, someone who had been through the hurt and suffered the loss. Although I could respect his perspective and his words, I made the choice for it to *break* me. After all, I was already shattered—I just consciously decided to give in to the brokenness. Because I gave myself over to being fully broken, and I didn't care, I was becoming part of what I was not.

During this, my darkest time, my mom didn't have a clue as to what was going on in my heart. She just did what was best, she held onto me and prayed over me.

Depression Hurts Physically

Something I learned during this time is that depression truly hurts in a really painful, physical way. It doesn't just hurt mentally; it is a full physical pain that runs through the body. I remember lying in bed with my legs and arms hurting so bad that I could hear the voices in my head say, "You would be better off if they were just cut off. Better yet, you would be better off if you just died."

I never gave in to those thoughts because I knew where they

were coming from, but the pain was so real, so intense, that I understood why people kill themselves. It isn't from being sad or rejected, but they *physically hurt,* and if someone isn't trained to fight those whispering evil voices, how can they survive the attack? I knew what was going on because of my upbringing and because of that, I was able to fight the attacks. But even still I was only human, and a broken human at that. If it wasn't for God, I am sure I would have lost; however, it was only God's grace that got me past everything. Despite the attacks and the fact that I knew God was my only hope, I still chose to be angry with Him for a long time. I remember praying to Him: "I still believe in You, but I am not talking to You." I prayed that prayer many times to my Father.

I couldn't even make it to church services during this time, and it was hard to even believe in prayer. Yes, I was sure God heard me, but I felt that God had turned His head away from me. As a result, my prayers seemed like just another thought or wish.

It was hard to be around other believers, to admit how much I hurt, because the more I thought about Abiah, the more my heart felt like it was breaking all over again. Despite my depressed feelings, what I truly needed was prayer—like I had never needed it so desperately before.

When I was finally ready to come back to God, He was able to release me from the attacks and the doubt. I was even able to get off all the medicine. The worst part about anti-depressants is that they mask the issue. No matter what, you eventually will have to go through the pain, the loss, the hurt, and the attack. You cannot mask it; you cannot run from it forever. They are a useful tool for getting us through, but eventually problems must be dealt with—and there is no better way to deal with problems than with God on your side. Years later when I got completely off of the anti-depressants, it was if I had to live the loss all over again, and if it wasn't for God, I would have ended up in an insane asylum.

> What then shall we say to these things? If God *is* for us, who *can be* against us? (Romans 8:31)

> You are of God, little children, and have overcome them, because He who is in you is greater than he who is in the world. (1 John 4:4)

> "No weapon formed against you shall prosper, And every tongue *which* rises against you in judgment You shall condemn. This *is* the heritage of the servants of the Lord, And their righteousness *is* from Me," Says the Lord. (Isaiah 54:17)

Endless Struggles

Not only does depression hurt, but it creates chaos throughout your entire body. A few months after Abiah passed, I started getting itchy all over. I was so itchy I would scratch my skin to the point of bleeding, and even then I couldn't get the itch to go away. I had sores, strawberries, and scratch marks all over my body and even on my head, hiding under my hair. When I went to the dermatologist, I really believed I had some illness that was causing the problem. However, I found out it wasn't a specific illness but from the trauma. The dermatologist inquired if I had been through something traumatic, and after I told him yes, he explained that when we go through something such as I did, the brain stops producing a hormone the skin needs, causing the extreme itching I was experiencing. Crazy—I would have never known.

When I finally went back to work, my biggest issue was driving to and from work. I had panic attacks daily and constantly. As I would drive to work, I would watch the yellow lines on the road and think, "I am that much closer to where I need to be." It was hard when I drove alone. I would go into hyperventilating attacks nonstop, taking in so much oxygen that my ears, face, and fingers would go numb. I think that happens right before passing out, but thankfully I didn't ever pass out behind the wheel. I don't think I would be here now if I had passed out while driving fast down a highway. God is good and He protected me, even when I wasn't calling upon Him.

Of course, it didn't help to promote my healing that I was angry with God. My anger allowed other attacks to take place. When you allow one sin—like misplaced anger—into your life, you open up to many more, getting weaker and weaker—becoming easier prey.

On the next page is a poem I wrote years later to express my feelings at that dark time of my life.

Young and pregnant
With a baby boy,
Knowing he will be raised alone
But getting ready for his home.

As I held him in my arms
Lord, I cried out to You.
As I held him in my arms
Sorry for the pain you knew.

Why, oh why,
Did he have to die?
Lord, tell me why, oh why,
Did he have to go?

Lord, You know
And Lord, You were there.
Give me hope
To know that You care.

So tell me, Lord
Why, oh why
Did I have to cry?
And why, oh why
Did he have to die?

Angels filled the room the day—
The day You carried him away.
I cried out to You,
Sorry for the pain you knew.

Wishing then, my heart could beat
For both you and for me.
Knowing you were going home,
But I was not letting go.

Looking back now I see, Lord,
The life You gave just for me.
Not knowing then what You knew,
All the pain he went through.

So tell me, God,
Why, oh why
Did Your Son have to die?
And why, oh why?
But for our life.

You gave Your Son
So we might live,
A gift I could not give.
But oh, Lord, You did.

So tell me, God,
Why, oh why
Did Your Son have to die?
And why, oh why?
But for our life.

Lord, you knew the *why*,
So I give you my gift back.
With a broken heart I cry.

Here is my why:
I give it all to You.
Mend this broken heart
And make it new.

The following poem was sent to us from either the funeral home or cemetery along with Abiah's picture. It still touches my heart.

"God looked around His garden
and He found an empty place,
He then looked down upon this earth,
and saw your tired face.
He put His arms around you
and lifted you to rest.
God's garden must be beautiful,
He always takes the best.
He knew that you were suffering,
He knew you were in pain.
He knew that you would never
get well on earth again.
He saw the road was getting rough
and the hills were hard to climb.
So He closed your weary eyelids,
and whispered, "Peace be thine."
It broke our hearts to lose you
but you didn't go alone.
For part of us went with you
the day God called you home."
(Author Unknown)

Precious Time

From the start of my pregnancy, I never thought about an abortion or an adoption. I wanted this baby, and I loved him from the start. My friend had a miscarriage, and she told me that her pain and loss could never measure up to mine. I look at it like this: Yes, I did get very attached just as any mother would. The moment I found out I was pregnant was the moment the feelings of love and bonding took place for me.

I am grateful for the days I did get to spend with Abiah. Mothers who have miscarriages never get to meet their babies—and that in itself is a different kind of awful pain—but I know they feel grief and loss, just as I did. It was not easy to lose a baby that I love so much, but I would not have changed any part of Abiah's life—it was all God's plan. So yes, I do see others' hurts, and I know their pain.

Having my son was no decision I even thought about; I just knew I was going to have him. The only decision I made was to fully trust in God and know that I am forgiven of all my sins. I know this because I simply asked.

If every parent would just look at their child and realize how God has blessed them with that life then I think many more would truly understand how great it is to be called *Mommy* or *Daddy*. If everyone would just treat their child as if it was their child's last day on earth, more people would see that the movie they are watching or the game that is on TV is not important. Pay attention when your child is trying to show you something—the little things are important to our chil-

These were some of Abiah's things. The special miracle cloth was something we placed in his bed; it was prayed over. The socks were way too big on him, but we put them on to keep him warm. The cassette was one we played in his room. I took the cords from his monitor and his blood pressure cuff. I never got to brush his hair with the brush, and he never got to use his binkie or play with his bear. The things I still have are small, but those things will be held in my heart forever.

dren, and that is what really matters. How I miss so many things about Abiah—his voice, his cry, the changing of the few diapers that I got to change. (I didn't care how dirty they were.) Children are a gift loaned to us by God for a little while, and you never know how long. I never knew until the final day that Abiah would truly be taken from me. A person never thinks about reality until it hits like a brick, and that brick was still attached to the house when it hit me.

So many children are lost every day. Many people don't view the loss as a reality because they never had to live it firsthand. But, loss does happen. We see on the news where children pass from some unforeseen accident or go missing or are ill—children should outlive their parents! What if this happened to just one child you know? What if that child was your own? Yes, it does happen—children do die, and oh, how it hurts! It hurts so bad I could never describe the pain and loss.

People need to see how important it is to show love and take every minute of the day seriously. Don't keep wasting time away in the monotony of daily life. I don't even like to think of how many children died while my son was in the hospital. I never thought that really happened until I lived it myself.

Many say everything happens for a reason and I believe that, but that's the last thing I wanted to hear in the midst of my grief. I wish that no one would ever have to go through the heartbreak from the loss of a child, but we live in a fallen and imperfect world. We must lean on God's plan and His faithfulness in the midst of overwhelming strife and woe.

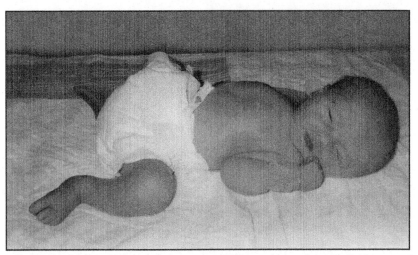

Christian Abiah Cobb before his surgery. What a perfect face! He had a ton of wires hooked up to him, but my brother removed what he could with Photoshop. Thank you, Sean; you are a good big brother.

**In loving memory of
Christian Abiah Cobb
(Little Abiah)
July 15, 1999 – August 10, 1999**

Chapter Nine

The Horrible Disease

¹ To everything there is a season,
A time for every purpose under heaven:
² A time to be born, And a time to die;
A time to plant, And a time to pluck what is planted;
³ A time to kill, And a time to heal;
A time to break down, And a time to build up;
⁴ A time to weep, And a time to laugh;
A time to mourn, And a time to dance;
Ecclesiastes 3:1-4

Shortly after my son passed, my mom told me an awful secret. One day while I was making lunch for the both of us, she said, "I have something to show you, but you cannot tell anyone. You have to promise. If you tell, I will not ever trust you again."

Because of our bond and relationship, I told her I would keep the secret—although now I wish I would not have remained silent. Telling this secret might have saved her life, but now it is too late.

The secret was that she had a lump in her breast. This lump wasn't any ordinary lump—it was the size of my fist or a grapefruit! My mom then told me if the lump was what she thought it was—breast cancer—then she was already dead. I freaked out when she told me this secret. I told her not to drink caffeine or eat any sugar and that I would monitor everything she ate. I felt like the lump had to do with how she was eating, and if I could watch what she ate, I could then help her heal. I was grasping at straws.

Why, God?

Throughout this time, all I could think was "Why, God? Why would you take my son and now my mom?" I couldn't think of getting through life without my mom. This secret that I promised to keep tormented me every day for a year. Still reeling from the shock of Abiah's death, and now my mother's silent illness, I was in no mental shape to argue with her or to convince her to seek help. All the while I kept this awful secret, my mom refused to go to the doctor. She was deathly afraid of doctors, and she didn't want anyone to know about her lump.

One day Mom called me while I was at work. She was crying because she couldn't get up. It had been one year since she told me about this secret, and because I kept my word, I rushed to my mom's aid. I was at the point that I couldn't keep the secret any longer; I was scared for her life. I held a meeting with my brother and told him everything. We then called my Aunt Janet, who was related on my dad's side of the family through marriage. She was the only one that we knew who would be strong enough in character that my mom wouldn't say no to, and they were close friends. My mom and Aunt Janet were actually the best of friends—my mom was blessed to have many best friends, true friends, who were very good to her.

Diagnosis

My aunt drove from Texas to Oklahoma to help us out. When she arrived in town, she was successful at talking my mom into going to the doctor. The doctor we found on late notice was awful—he was rude with no feeling when he spoke and no calming bedside manner that you would expect from a physician. He told me that day that my mom didn't have a chance, and he sent her directly to the hospital. At the hospital we were told that my mom had cancer and only six months to live, if that. God is in control of our time here. Doctors can estimate, but only God knows, and everything is in His timing. My mom lived another four years after this diagnosis.

My mom's cancer started in the breast, went to the hip, then the spine. From there it spread throughout her body. What ended up taking my mom's life was when the cancer reached her brain. The doctors explained that the cancer in her brain was like weeds, anywhere it touched it produced a tumor. When my mom passed, she had over eleven tumors in her brain—one was even the size of a quarter and located in the part of the brain that affected her motor skills.

My mom went to many chemo treatments and radiation. The doctors even tried doing the gamma knife procedure on her, but the laser broke down while my mom was on the table. The doctors said they had never had it break before. She already had the halo drilled into her head, and the doctors couldn't do anything else. She went through all of that pain for nothing.

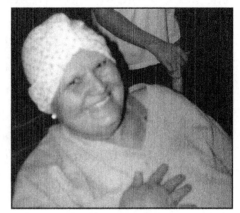

Mom remained joyful throughout her cancer treatments.

More Bad News

About a year after my mom was diagnosed with cancer, she and Aunt Janet had decided to go on a trip to the beach. (This was before the cancer made it to her brain, and she was still able to move freely.) When they were about to leave, my aunt called to cancel because she kept passing out. Aunt Janet had to be rushed to the hospital herself where doctors discovered a tumor in her brain the size of a golf ball. My aunt went through brain surgery only for it to grow back as quickly as the symptoms first began. At this time Aunt Janet swore she would never have brain surgery again, and she passed shortly after.

My mom felt so guilty. She never could understand why Janet would be taken before her.

Final Days

The week before my mom passed, I ended up moving back in with her so I could be her caregiver. I didn't want her passing in a hospital, but I also didn't want her to be alone. She never wanted to be on hospice, but I think it was the fear of the word and what it stood for, rather than the help she would receive. In the end, we had to bring hospice in because I was working half days, and my brother was helping, but one of us just couldn't always be there. Hospice filled those gaps in my mom's care, and I thank the Lord for them; they were amazing.

Broken Again

The day my mom passed, I overslept and didn't wake up in time to give her the pain medicine that she needed. It was a simple eye drop that would get into her bloodstream and help with pain. When I went into my mom's room late that morning, her eyes were open, the TV was still on from the night before (the way she liked it at night), and a single tear was coming down her face. She couldn't speak, but I knew she was in pain. I cry to this day every time I recall her lying there in pain—it was my fault, and this tore me down even farther than where I was. I blame myself for that tear, the pain, and the hurt she must have felt during that last morning.

I went in to work when hospice got there that day, but I ended up leaving early because I wanted to be with my mom. I had a bad feeling. That morning hospice told us she had about six weeks to live. A few hours later their estimate went down to four weeks, then one week, and then later that same day she passed. Once again, only God knows our time.

Heaven Bound

Before my mom left her earthly home, she was lying in her bed with her preacher friend by her side. I was standing at the doorway, with the preacher's wife, who was another one of my mom's best friends. As I was standing at the doorway, I was silently yelling at God in my head. "God, if you are going to take my mom, then take her, quit putting her through this pain. If not, then heal her soon, just please quit letting her go

The day of my mom's funeral. My older brother, Sean, and I are standing in front of our mom's house where we grew up. I lived in that house for nineteen years of my life, and I still miss it; it was a house of peace.

through this pain!" I was yelling at the top of my thoughts; I was so angry and hurt. Not only did I lose my sweet baby, but now my mom. How much of my heart was God going to take?

As I was finishing up my angry prayer, the pastor's wife looked at me and said, "God wants me to tell you something: your mom is not in pain; angels have filled this room. Your mom is with me right now, and I am preparing her. She is not in pain."

I started crying right then because I realized that God heard every word I just yelled at him and had sent me a comforting response. It felt good to know my mom wasn't hurting, and God knew that I needed to hear that. Mom's eyes were closed, and she wasn't responding. I knew everything that the pastor's wife had just told me was straight from God, my Father. My mom wasn't here on earth.

Later that night, my mom opened her eyes for the first time since earlier that morning. Her gurgle stopped for a quick second, and I thought that maybe God was giving me a miracle and healing her. She looked over at me, then looked at my brother, and then took her last breath. I was holding her hand when she left. I started to cry, but I felt her in the room for a split second, as if she was watching us, and I could hear her say, "Don't cry; I am okay," and then she left to be with my Father in heaven.

Funeral

The day of the funeral my mom had received more flow-

My mom's grave

ers than the funeral home had ever seen. In fact, they had so many arrangements that they filled her room and spilled down the halls. They even had to close off the two rooms next to hers to fill those rooms with flowers. It even got to the point that they started delivering the flowers to the graveside because they were completely out of room for any more flowers to come in. It was beautiful, seeing the love people had for my mom. I just wish I would have taken the time to thank all of them. Everything everyone did meant so much to us, and I messed up by not sending out thank you cards. We appreciate the love everyone gave to Mom, and for being there for us during this time in our lives. To this day I don't understand why I didn't write thank you cards. A part of me

Thank you mom for all you've done,
You encouraged us by being strong.
Your smile made everything alright,
Not having you will seem all wrong.

The three of us have been so close,
Being just two will be very tough.
Our time together ended too soon,
Precious Moments ...
there were never enough.

My brother wrote this for the funeral. Our mom had loved and collected Precious Moments figurines, so it was a fitting memorial for her life.

felt like if I did, it was accepting the fact that she was really gone, and that by not writing the cards, it kept a part of her legacy open. If I wrote them, it was closing the doors. I know that sounds weird, but inside that is all I could feel.

Her Obituary

Joyce E. Cobb has gone to rest in the arms of

Jesus after a long battle with cancer. She joins her mother Dorothy Schmitt, her father Sullivan W. Ives, and her infant grandson Christian Abiah Cobb, who preceded her into new life. Throughout her struggle, she never wavered in her faith and continued to give glory to God, praising Him for His goodness and mercy. Joyce retired from her job where she was a dutiful civil servant for over three decades. Joyce was an inspiration to all who knew and loved her; she faced each challenge life handed her with confidence in her Savior and determination to do God's will. She had the greatest laugh in the world; she was loving, kind, generous, funny, and intelligent. She was devoted to her God, her children, her family, and her friends. Her sweet smile could brighten the darkest day and her laughter could fill a room and make everyone around her feel better. In her darkest hours if you asked how she was, she would smile and say, "I'm just fine."

Chapter Ten

Married for the Wrong Reasons

There is a way that seems right to a man,
But its end is the way of death.
Proverbs 14:12

A year after my son passed, and shortly after my mom told me about her secret tumor, I was still on high doses of anti-depressants. I admit that I was afraid to be alone—I didn't have someone who was a father to me here on earth, I was about to lose my mom, I had already lost my son—I just wanted someone to be with me, to love me, and to not leave. This was when I met my first husband, John.

Wedding Day

Two weeks after we started dating, John asked me to marry him. I said yes, knowing it wasn't right, and because my mom was against the marriage, we went and secretly got married one day during our lunch hour. I should have known that if you have to hide something from the ones who love you the most, then it is probably not what you should be doing.

The day we got married I was wearing black pants, and he was wearing jeans. During our vows we were laughing so much that the officiant stopped and asked us if we were related or something. Obviously we weren't, but we didn't take any part of our marriage seriously, from the moment we said "I do" all the way to the moment I stood before the judge with a divorce decree.

My mom didn't want me to marry John because she said he wasn't my type—not because something was wrong with him—she just knew me. My mom knew that the anti-depressants were messing with my judgment and personality; she feared that when I got off the anti-depressants that my new husband wouldn't be able to handle my strong-willed manner. She was right in every single way. She begged for me to wait to marry him until I was completely off of the medicine, but I didn't listen. I am not sure if I didn't listen to her sound judgment because I felt I would never get off the medicine, or if it was because I married him knowing we wouldn't last.

Our marriage was just a cover, a bandage to protect me from the pain that was to come. Anyone who has ever had a sore knows that sometimes we put bandages on to protect a wound, but sometimes that bandage causes more harm than good, allowing the sore to stay moist and not heal. In this case, I was trying to create healing before the hurt took place. I created a bandage that wasn't in God's plan for either of us.

Our Marriage

During our marriage we even had a running joke about when we would get divorced. It was funny at the time, but now that I look back I realize how sad it really was. I didn't take the institution of marriage seriously; I didn't look at marriage as a lasting part of my life. Being medicated and heartbroken, I looked at things differently than most, and I also had a wall that I protected myself with. This wall was a fake protector so that nothing could get through to my heart and so that nothing could further hurt me. This wall was built up around my life so it would be easy for me to walk away and not become too attached to anyone or anything.

During this marriage, I realized that life existed outside of my "Chris bubble." In my own private "Chris bubble," I believed that everyone was honest because I was honest. In my bubble, I believed that everyone was nice because I was nice; but I had a lot of growing up to do. During this marriage, I grew up.

John and I were too young to get married, and what's even worse is that we didn't know each other at all. Plenty of successful married couples come together at a young age, but those are couples who take marriage seriously; who take the time and effort to get to know one another; who invest their lives into their spouse and actually fall in love. If we would have waited to get married, my life would have been different in many ways. Although it was not the marriage I was meant to have, some aspects of it I would not change for anything. As I said, I grew up immensely during this marriage.

Good Times & Bad

I will not go into too much detail about my ex-husband because I do believe he has changed a lot and is still changing for the better. Plus, every story has two sides, and I am sure he has his own story he tells. I will admit that I was very cold-hearted in this marriage. I didn't allow for him to cry around me. He did nothing wrong there; it was because of what I had been through. I looked at crying as a sign of weakness because of my experience with Caleb and because of the loss I went through with my son. I looked at those who cried and thought that they better really have something to cry about—otherwise, all respect was lost. I felt that I knew what real tears and real hurt were and that if this was not his experience, he had no reason to be upset. This was not fair of me to hold over John's head, and because of that, he was never allowed to show emotions with me.

One thing I would never change about our marriage was that while we were married, we were blessed with a beautiful son. We named him a unique name that means "he who God protects." I like unique names and have always believed that a name can be a blessing or a curse. I wanted my son to be blessed by his name. I believe that when people speak his name they are speaking a covering of blessing over him. He is protected. It could have stemmed from the loss of Abiah, but I feared a lot over my new son's safety throughout my pregnancy and his early life.

Darkness

During our marriage I had a gun pulled on me twice. I also came within seconds of losing my life completely. A gunman held my baby and me hostage in our own home because of some illicit activities that were going on behind my back. My husband knew I would leave if I knew what was happening, and so he kept it a secret until the night we were held hostage.

I remember that night sharply, perfectly. It was sleeting outside, and our son was a newborn. A large guy sat outside our bedroom door, threatening me and not letting us out of the room. His gun was loaded and close to me as he spoke. When he shut us in the room, I sat at the end of the bed trying to figure out how to escape. My car was in the garage, and to get to the garage I would have to go through him. I thought about going out the window, but then I was putting my son in danger, being outside in the cold weather on foot. I sat there and prayed. Later when I found out the entire story, I sat at the end of the bed praying, "God, this isn't the life you called for me to live." I was ready to leave. I started to pack, and God told me to wait, not to leave yet. I trusted God, and I stayed with the promise from my husband that he would never get involved in that lifestyle again.

God protected me all through that marriage. So many things

took place, but God had his covering over my son and me. I thank the Lord for His continuing love.

The Beginning of the End

Even after the hostage situation, I continued to hear God saying I was to stay in this relationship. Many people told me during our marriage that my husband was cheating on me, but I wasn't sure. He was still involved in many things that I was unaware of, and it was difficult to trust him, but I remained married to him, convinced that it was what I was called to do. I was married, and God does not support divorce, except where there is marital unfaithfulness. At the time, I could not prove that my husband was unfaithful, so I continued to pray and seek God's leading.

One night, my husband came home mysteriously in the middle of the night, and I prayed this specific prayer: "God, I know you didn't raise me to be treated like this, to have this kind of a marriage. God, this isn't what I want. Please, God, change his heart or let this marriage end."

A few weeks later my husband started threatening that he was going to move out. I kept telling him that if he moved out, we wouldn't be able to work out our problems and that we would end up divorced. This was the only time I actually fought for my marriage, and it wasn't even for me—it was for my son, who was now five years old and needed his father.

One day when I was driving with my son in the back seat, my husband called. Our son heard us arguing about him moving out. When I finally hung up the phone, my son said, "Mom, if Dad wants to move out, let him go. We will be just fine without him."

I ruefully said, "Baby, I know I will be just fine without him, but will you?"

After I asked my son this question he responded, "Yes, Mom, I will be just fine, and when you get remarried, I will call him Dad, too."

The hair on my arms stood straight up. I knew God was speaking to me through my son. He was way too young to speak to me like this! He was just a little boy who knew nothing of marriage, divorce, or remarriage. I knew God was finally releasing me from this marriage.

The Call

On New Year's Eve I received a phone call from a prophet that I hadn't spoken with in over twenty years. She was given my phone number through our former pastor. She called me to say that God had told her to pass a message on to me. This was the message: "Your husband is walking the fence. He wants the world and he wants you, but God told him he can't have both—he can either have the world, or you." She then went on to say that I wasn't to have union with him any longer. This was the message from the Lord that I had been waiting to hear. Later that night when my husband came to pick up his stuff, I told him what the prophet said and he was in shock. A few days later, he sent me an e-mail that admitted that he had been cheating. Upon hearing this news, I left work to go pick up our son. While I was driving, crying, and praying, I felt God tell me that I could stay with him and He would bless me, or I could leave and He would bless me; but no matter my choice, He was going to bless me. That was the moment I was done. The burden was lifted. My marriage was over. I was not condemned; I was released. I let my husband go, and he let me go. We were married seven and a half years.

After Christmas that year, my husband made the final decision to leave. My son and I took down all of the holiday decorations, and instead of putting our house back to normal, we spent time rearranging every single thing to make it look different. I took down pictures with John in them, and I did whatever I could to get any thought of him completely out. I packed up all of his stuff and put it all in boxes. As the Beyoncé song says, "Everything he owned went in the box to the left." I tried to change the look of the house by changing the way we had everything in the house, from furniture to decorations to knick-knacks. It was finally time for a fresh start.

God was true to His word, as always. God blessed our divorce—it was smooth and quick. We were divorced within thirty days of filing. Thank you, Jesus. God worked through it all. I give God the glory for the blessings in my life.

> And we know that all things work together for
> good to those who love God, to those who are
> the called according to His purpose.
> (Romans 8:28)

The year John left was the biggest blessing that ever happened in my life. It was not just a blessing to me, but to him as well. We were not meant for each other. I believe that by getting married in the first place, we stepped out of God's plan, and because of that, we had to go through a hard time in life with each other. However, God used those hard times to His glory and still blessed us with an amazing son. God is good. Don't get me wrong, I do not believe God desires or wants divorces for his children, but God simply had other plans for both of us. In order to grow in His love and plan, we had to do so separately.

After John left, my son said, "See how peaceful it is now?" It was God speaking again through my son, just confirming that it was all going to be okay.

However, when John left, he left us in a bad place financially. None of our bills were paid. Everything was behind, and we had no money in our accounts. I had to take out a loan from my brother to catch up the house and car payments and the utility bills; I also had to take out a loan from my brother so I could pay for my divorce. God was faithful in providing, and I was able to pay my brother back in less time than what I expected.

My ex-husband is now married and I believe his wife is perfect for him. He seems to have changed a lot and that was always my prayer for his life. I didn't want him to be out of our son's life, and because of that, he needed to change his ways. God has been moving in his life, and I praise Him for that.

He seems to be a good dad and a better person since our divorce. I have no bad feelings towards him—God worked in my heart and a full healing took place within. I pray blessings over him and his wife and their marriage.

Looking back at our marriage, I feel it is important to restate that I was not the best wife, either. I do not wish to give the impression that I was faithfully praying for my husband to change because I was already made perfect. In truth, I made plenty of mistakes, especially at the end of our marriage. During that time I allowed anger to enter my heart, and due to the anger, I said many things that should have never come out of my mouth. I do believe that God had a lot of work to do on me as a wife. I was quick to build walls and quick to walk out on the drop of a hat. God used this experience to grow me in many immeasurable ways.

Transition

I was thirty years old when I went through my divorce, which was the same age my mom was when her husband left her. When I realized this, the fear of dying alone started to creep in for a moment, but that fear was covered by my actions. I started going out every weekend that my son was visiting his dad, and when I partied, I really partied. I drank a lot, and I started smoking. I was dating and having fun, but I was not interested in marriage again—I had sworn off the idea of it all together.

Having regained my life and sense of independence, I was

going through a major rebellion. I was on speaking terms with God, but I was only a part-time Christian. I needed God and asked for His help, but when things were going well, I was doing my own thing.

Truthfully, it was a pure miracle that I lived through that time of my life. I was smoking, drinking, and crashing at friends' houses because I didn't believe in drinking and driving; however, I would let my friends be completely plastered when I got into cars with them. When I went out, I would

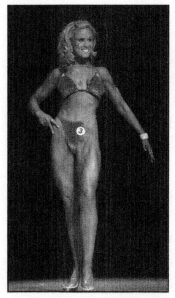

I won second place at a show for my figure.

drink obscene amounts of alcohol mixed with energy drinks, a dangerous combination. On top of that, I was smoking, so that when I would wake up the next morning my heart would be beating too fast. I am surprised my heart didn't give out under the pressure. Unfortunately, I didn't care about preserving my life. I was reckless; I had been through so much in my young life that I was pretty much done and living on the edge. The only thing I did care about was my little boy.

I went through an aftershock from the divorce that included much more than drinking and smoking. I was having fun. I went skydiving, which I had always wanted to try, and I started doing figure body building shows. These are not

After my divorce, I did something I had wanted to do for years – skydive!

necessarily bad things, but I wasn't anywhere that I needed to be in my life. I was promoted at work and had the perfect job that made a lot of money for us. I was a business professional during the day, but I lived my life for me and not for God, so everything was a big mess.

I was living for myself for the moment, something that is easy to do when you go through a hard blow and must transition through life's changes. However, as a single mother who was brought up to know the Lord, my priorities were certainly focused incorrectly. Thankfully, this season in my life only lasted a few months, and I never did any of this in front of my son. I refused to drink or smoke in front of him, but eventually it caught up to me. One day he caught me out back smoking, and he cried because I had taught him that smoking was dangerous. My heart broke when he cried, but it wasn't enough to change my ways. I wasn't acting like myself or thinking clearly, so I continued to drink and smoke, but never in front of him. Like I said, thankfully that phase in my life was short-lived, and I do not miss any part it. It might have been fun during the moment, but God had things that were much greater in store for me.

My job was to be a mom, a wife, and a servant to God. I was made to live as a light for others to see God's glory, but at that time I was choosing destruction over life.

> [14] "You are the light of the world. A city that is set on a hill cannot be hidden. [15] Nor do they light a lamp and put it under a basket, but on a lampstand, and it gives light to all who are in the house. [16] Let your light so shine before men, that they may see your good works and glorify your Father in heaven."
> (Matthew 5:14-16)

The Road to Prison

While I was going through this rebellious stage, God told me I would go into prison to minister. When I heard this call, it scared me because I never wanted to go into prison. I was afraid of the request. Would I be visiting? Or would my new lifestyle lead me to be incarcerated? When I thought of prisons, I thought of darkness, violence, and the type of people I did not want to surround myself with, so I blew Him off and rebuked the calling. But God is good. I had no clue my perspective would ever change, but years later God would change my heart.

Leaving Rebellion Behind

Life is one decision after another. You make a decision, and once you make it, you can't change it. People often ask me if I would have ever changed what has happened to me, and as I look back, I see that without these steps in my life, I wouldn't be where I am now. God allowed my decision to take me to a place where He wanted me. It might not have been the way He would have chosen, but nevertheless, He used it for His glory and my good. He allowed my decisions to take me to my knees, which led to a place of redemption and freedom in His arms. Without Him I would still be lost, broken, and in darkness.

It took years to get past the hurt of being rejected and cheated on, but God healed me. Only God can turn that kind of pain into glory. It's not God's will for us to go through these trials in life, but when we don't listen to him, we get ourselves into messes, and messes are never easy to clean up.

I know now that to really live for God we have to fully surrender everything. God is the maker of all that is good. His desire is for us to inherit His treasures. Why do we fight to release it all? So many do as I once did, and we try to hold onto things thinking that we are in control. There are two forces in this world: if God isn't in control, then the other is, and I don't want that force to have a hold on my life. I lived that life—it may seem fun for a short time, but the outcome is darkness. I continue to choose light, and I want to be God's vessel living fully in Him.

> ²⁴ Then Jesus said to His disciples, "If anyone desires to come after Me, let him deny himself, and take up his cross, and follow Me. ²⁵ For whoever desires to save his life will lose it, but whoever loses his life for My sake will find it. ²⁶ For what profit is it to a man if he gains the whole world, and loses his own soul? Or what will a man give in exchange for his soul? ²⁷ For the Son of Man will come in the glory of His Father with His angels, and then He will reward each according to his works." (Matthew 16:24-27)

Chapter Eleven
My Gifts

Every good gift and every perfect gift is from above,
and comes down from the Father of lights,
with whom there is no variation or shadow of turning.
James 1:17

One day in 2008 one of my friends came over to visit like she always did, but that day something was different. She asked that I meet one of her guy friends and mentioned that we would be perfect for each other. She had never asked this of me before. I told her to show me a picture, and when she did, I told her no immediately. Not because of the guy's looks—he was very handsome—but because he was wearing a uniform. You see, I had a rule that I wouldn't date anyone in the military. My dad had been in the military, and he cheated on my mom. Based on that experience, I assumed that all military men cheated, so little did I know.

After I told my friend no, she begged for me to give him a

chance and to just talk to him. Because of her persistence, I told her that I would talk to him, but that was as far as it would ever go. Again, so little did I know.

Just Talking

We started talking via online messaging because he was in Iraq for military duty. My mindset was that he was safe to talk to because he was far away, so it was like he wasn't even real because I probably would never see him in person. We started talking, and I told him right away that I would never get married again—that it wasn't even up for discussion. We talked a lot of times through the entire night after my son went to bed.

During our conversations, we started noticing that many things about us just came together. God sure is funny. You see, I am one who always prays for signs, and through my frequent requests for a sign, God shows me things. It's almost like our little thing we have with each other, my Father and I. When I started talking to this guy, God told me I would marry him. I laughed at that because, in my head, that was never going to happen again.

And here is where God starts to show his sense of humor. This guy's name is Christopher, and mine is Christina, but we both go by Chris. His brother's name is Sean, and my brother's name is Sean. His brother's birthday is two days before my brother's birthday. And here is the kicker: his birthday is three days before my birthday, the same day as my mom's. Wow, God, could you give me any more signs?

My mom was my hero, and she isn't here any longer so God gave me this gift, a precious gift. There were many other signs along the way, but these were the biggest of them all.

When he finally got home from his tour in Iraq, we had been talking so much that we knew each other although we had never met. Through our long-distance relationship, we fell in love with each other's hearts—not our looks, not the sound of our voices, but who we really were. Add that to God's signs, and we knew we were meant for each other. We ended up getting married about a year after we met, but this time around

Chris and Chris on the day of his brother's graduation.

I had a real wedding with a small group of our families and friends. It was perfect; the only thing missing was my mom.

Married

Guy Chris (as I affectionately call my husband) was 25 when we met. He had never been married, and he never had any children. He was excited to bring my son on as his own, and he was also ready to have a baby together. Even I was excited to have another. When we were talking about having children, he said that if we ever had a daughter he wanted to name her Alexandria. I was not a big fan of that name and said NO WAY. He let it go, and I was glad because I didn't want to name my daughter Alexandria. As I have proved with my sons, I prefer unique, meaningful names, and Alexandria seemed far too common.

We tried to get pregnant, but it just wasn't happening. I started to think that I had done something wrong and that God wasn't going to bless us with another child. That is when God spoke to me about my daughter. He told me that when I had a girl that I was to name her Alexandria. I agreed to this, and at that moment I knew I was going to have a daughter.

The next day was Mother's Day. I took a pregnancy test, and to my surprise it came back positive. Guy Chris was so excited, and his excitement increased when I told him that when we had our daughter we were to name her Alexandria. I told him that was going to be her name, it was God's direction, and I knew we were having a daughter. He kept saying, "No, if you don't want to name her that, I want to do what we both like."

I knew that I had to keep my promise to God, so I insisted on the name Alexandria, knowing in my heart that we were having a little girl.

Before our first checkup, Guy Chris kept saying that I was going to have twins. How he knew, I don't know, but sure enough, when we went to the doctor for our checkup, we noticed two babies. Our joy quickly turned to concern when the doctor was checking on the babies, and he said that he thought I was losing one of them. It was a medical scenario called vanishing twin syndrome. I left there so upset, but my husband kept saying, "Don't worry; our babies are fine. We are not losing either baby."

Guy Chris was right. When we went back for our follow-up visit, both babies were okay. Later we found out we were having a boy and a girl. The boy was my surprise because I already knew one was a baby girl. God is so good, and our babies are blessings from above, our gifts from God. When our oldest son found out we were having a boy and girl, he said, "Mom, God is giving you another boy because he took your other one."

I started crying the moment he told me that. My oldest is a true gift, so blessed with the Holy Spirit.

> [3] Behold, children *are* a heritage from the Lord,
> The fruit of the womb is a reward. [4] Like ar-

rows in the hand of a warrior, So are the children of one's youth. [5] Happy is the man who has his quiver full of them; (Psalm 127:3-5a)

When our twins were born, we named our daughter Alexandria, as promised, and our son Lathan, which means "he that God has given." Thank you, Lord, for my gifts—all six of my blessings, Little Abiah and my mom in heaven, Guy Chris, our oldest son, and our twins, Lathan and Alexandria. Of course, I can't forget our two dogs who are part of our family as well: Optimus and Marshal.

Chapter Twelve

Refuse to Stay Broken

*² By this we know that we love the children of God,
when we love God and keep His commandments.
³ For this is the love of God, that we keep His commandments.
And His commandments are not burdensome.
⁴ For whatever is born of God overcomes the world.
And this is the victory that has overcome the world—our faith.
⁵ Who is he who overcomes the world,
but he who believes that Jesus is the Son of God?*
1 John 5:2-5

Our twins were around six months old when Guy Chris was sent back overseas, but this time to Afghanistan. During the time Guy Chris was gone, God got ahold of me and told me once again that I would go into prison to minister. I once again became scared and refused the request as if it was the devil lying to me. Finally God said, "You will go on your own or I will send you." I felt like Jonah in the belly of the whale. If I didn't do what I was told, God was going to make sure I fulfilled His request. I knew I had better obey.

The Class

I started calling around to see how I could get into prison to minister. This is when I met my good friend, Gena. She was teaching a class that I needed to attend in order to get into prison ministry. God opened the doors perfectly, and I took her class, which happened to be designed for people who had addictions, something I didn't struggle with. I felt like it was going to be a big waste of time; however, I had to take the class to get badged so I could go into prison to teach.

Despite my misgivings, this class changed my life. It took us a year to get through it all, and I was the only one who ended up graduating that time around, but God knew how much I needed it. I realized later that God sending me to prison to minister wasn't just for the incarcerated women, but it was also for me. I grew up the year I went through that training and even during the time that I spent with the ladies in prison. God became a priority in my life, my desire. He was what I wanted, and I wasn't going to quit until I reached where God was calling me to be in my life.

Continued Obedience

Because I choose to obey God, my life is better all around. I have everything I have ever dreamed of and more. I have what God wants for me, and nothing can beat His desires for our lives. Because of God's faithfulness, I am a better mom to my beautiful children, my precious gifts. I am a better wife to Guy Chris, a better servant to my Father, and a better worker for the business God has called me to start. I give God the glory because without Him, nothing is possible.

Now my job is to pray that I raise my children up the way God has called and to obey His leading for their lives as well.

> Train up a child in the way he should go, And
> when he is old he will not depart from it.
> (Proverbs 22:6)

On September 7, 2014, at 2:18 p.m., my four-year-old son asked Jesus into his heart. The seed has been planted. Later that night his twin sister did the same. God is good, and nothing can compare to him and the grace He has given us. I would be lost and still broken if He didn't call unto me, but because of His grace, I live a life that is perfectly new and blessed in Him and by Him.

I spent years asking God why Abiah was taken from me when I would have loved and cared for him so completely. About two years ago, I realized that God didn't take Abiah away from me to hurt me. Rather, God protected him from the harm this world inflicted upon him in that hospital. God protected him from the pain that was given to him, something he never did anything to deserve. Because of the love God had for him, God stepped in and saved him from the pain. I love all of my children, and I now know that God loves them more than I could ever dream. I used to blame

God for taking my son. I was so angry! I was broken because of that anger, but God refused to let me stay broken. He took that brokenness and made me new and more beautiful than I could have ever become on my own. I have a purpose, a calling on my life.

Our children are our gifts on loan to us from God. One thing I learned years ago at a young age is to never ever take those gifts for granted because you never know when a hug could be the last hug or a kiss could be the last kiss. Hold them tight, love them, and teach them the right way. Don't let television, friends, or other outside forces teach your children, but rather live your life according to your purpose so that they may see a living testament of God's love. Pray that through your life they will see their dreams fulfilled in God's plan.

Forgiveness and God's Grace

Because of God's grace and love for me, I refuse to hold on to unforgiveness, I refuse to hold on to anger, I refuse to blame others for my mistakes, I refuse to live off of the past, and most of all I refuse to stay broken. God is my healer, my creator, and my everything. Through Him all of our scars can be turned into beauty marks, all of our hurts can be used to heal others, and all of our pain can be turned into His glory. Our only job is to allow God to do the work and to surrender our all.

I used to think that if I held on to everything I could control my life, but it was when I released my all that God was able to build me back up into a new creation, His vessel.

If you have hurt, sadness, or brokenness, God can heal you. All you have to do is be willing to lay it all down. Turn it all over to God, and remember most of all to love and to forgive. One thing I learned in my year of training was how to love past all offense and forgive even those who have hurt us and those who try to hurt us. Forgiveness is very important for healing and sometimes the only way to forgive is to pray for the people who hurt us.

> "But I say to you, love your enemies, bless those who curse you, do good to those who hate you, and pray for those who spitefully use you and persecute you..." (Matthew 5:44)

When we pray for those who despitefully use us, God can not only create something amazing within, but also show His light through us to others and we can shine brightly during the darkness.

That year of class brought healing to my life. God knew that all it was going to take was that one step of obedience to allow myself to grow up and to forgive all the hurt that took place in my past so that my future could be in God's will and not my own. As I get older I see that the things that brought me to complete brokenness are the things that God was able to use to create a new masterpiece. The pain that I went through was not in vain.

God is good, and I now have a friendship with my earthly dad; however, my Father is in heaven, He is my Dad, my God, and my King and I wouldn't change Him being my Father for anything. I give glory to my Father, for without Him I truly would be nothing but broken pieces.

His Continued Provision

God has been amazing throughout my life. Even when I didn't know He was there, He was. He moved me in every direction of His desire. I may have fought Him on many things, but I continually choose to believe, and in the end, He has won me, completely. I pray He never lets me go. It's so easy to walk away from Him, but every time I walk away, I feel empty. No matter what I try to fill the space with, nothing is as fulfilling as my God, my King.

In my life, God has opened doors for great jobs that were blessings along the way. My field of work is in marketing and advertising. In my most recent job, I was blessed continually in a way that only God could provide. I was there for close to ten years, and although I often wanted to leave, God kept telling me to wait—that the right time would come and He would let me know.

In December of 2013, my favorite boss was let go, and she was the one who stood behind me, backed me, and believed in me. When she was let go, I felt God telling me it was time to move on. I knew the time for change was upon me, and I was both excited and fearful. I didn't know where God wanted me to go—many jobs were offered, many opportunities arose, but my husband kept saying, "Chris, you need to start your own business." The thought of going off on my own and starting a business scared me—I wanted stability, and I wanted to know a paycheck was coming every month. I felt God telling me to have peace, but the thought still scared me.

When I began to contemplate my own company, my old boss was a blessing and stepped in to help me get started. God placed her in my life to move me from where I was to where I was supposed to be. She backed me all the way, but I knew God was telling me that she wouldn't be involved with the company for long; she was there for a season, and for that moment, she was exactly what I needed. God knew my needs, and He provided. Thank you, Jesus.

New Business, New Adventure

After some time debating over the new business, I had decided to move forward with it; however, I got stuck and it went nowhere. My husband was tired of me saying what I was going to do, but not moving towards growth. One day before church he said, "Chris, if you are starting a business, you need to pick a date and stick to it."

That night at church, God confirmed his words. The preacher flat-out said, "If you are starting a business, pick a date."

Could it get any clearer?! God has a sense of humor. I had never spoken with this minister, so I knew it was God, and so did my husband. The look he shot at me screamed I TOLD YOU SO!

I picked a date, and that act of obedience was exactly what was needed for planning. But no matter what opportunities came my way, God had me keep the business dealings squeaky clean. God wanted His hand in my business, and because of that He wanted everything to stay pure.

Leap of Faith

In September of 2013, God gave me my New Year's resolution early. He told me that the year of 2014 would be the year of obedience, and when I obeyed, I would be given everything I desire. I would be blessed. When I received that revelation, I knew it was going to be hard and I would be told to do something that would be scary, but I knew I had to obey.

At my job, in 2013, I was paid around $120,000, and third party vendors paid me an additional $50,000. I gave my notice at work on April 1, 2014, effectively leaving a job that provided nearly $200,000 annually to start my own marketing and advertising company. Most people thought I was crazy, especially the people at my former company. But I knew nothing was crazy when God was behind it. I had to take a leap of faith and follow His calling on my life. When I gave my notice, I was told I probably wouldn't be allowed back because I was suddenly considered a competitor, and on April 2nd I was asked to come give my exit interview. I was out of there, a place I had been working at for close to ten years.

God is good. That company was a blessing, and I do believe God blessed them through me. I felt as though in many ways I allowed myself to be used by God within the workings of that company. For my role, I was blessed as well; however, I do believe when God decided to remove His hand from that company, He showed me in many ways in confirmation that it was time. His hand was removed from there, and with that, He was taking me with Him.

Obedience

When God moved me to start my business, I was scared to obey, but I knew I had to. I knew this was in God's plan. God had even blessed me with a husband who supported this crazy plan. Guy Chris backed everything—even knowing we could lose our house if things didn't work out. He didn't care; he wanted me to follow what he knew I was supposed to do.

When I left to start our company—I say ours because it is God's, my husband's and mine—I had a millionaire customer who offered to invest in our company because he wanted me to leave the other place. He believed so strongly that he even pushed for me to start a business. I prayed a lot about whether or not we should use him as an investor. I knew with this investor we would have a guaranteed paycheck monthly, but God told me NO. God said, "That investor is not your god. He is not your provider. I AM."

Because I obeyed, I now have my heart's desire. I have more time for prayer and more time with my family, plus I have an amazing company called Square Compass Media. We have very large companies that we do work for, and we pray over the companies for whom we run advertisements. We pray blessings in everything we do: that every company that works with us will be blessed and become a blessing, that they know God's hand is behind them because they are working with us, and that we have been well trained to do what is needed for them. We run our business with ethics. We are honest, and we keep things pure in our work and that is something each and every client respects and loves about us. God is good.

I continually pray that I keep pure in everything I do with this company. I also help contract out people when I see they are in need of money. God has blessed us so that we can bless others. I give God the glory.

We have now (at the time of this book's publishing) been in business for over a year and a half, and God is still moving strongly with this company. If my company is to continue, that is solely in God's hands. I am to just trust Him and be obedient to His calling.

Obedience is an important part of our lives. When we are young, we are to obey our parents. When we get older and we hear and know God's voice, we are to obey Him. If we are obedient, we can then be moved into His inheritance, His blessings. It's when we do our own will that we move ourselves into a mess. I lived my own will for many years, and because of it, I went through a lot of hurt, heartache, and pain. Through God there is healing, life, blessing, and growth.

In my past, I can't say I was always doing the right thing; I have made many mistakes, but through those mistakes I have learned many valuable lessons and grown closer to my Creator. It's in our mistakes and failures that we become strong, but only if we learn and allow those times to teach us.

Closing

"For *as* the heavens are higher than the earth,
So are My ways higher than your ways, And
My thoughts than your thoughts." (Isaiah 55:9)

I didn't write this book to show who I am—I wrote this book to show who I was, and then who God *created*. God's creation is so much better than my own, better than anything I could ever dream.

I also didn't write this book to say "Look at me!" I wrote this book out of obedience—I knew God told me years ago that I would write a book. This book is to say "Wow! I have made many mistakes in my life, even after I came to Christ, and even as I serve Him now, I make plenty of mistakes; but through Christ I am a new creation. I am clean every morning, but to be cleansed I have to come to Him."

If you want to change your life and the way you look at things, if you want healing, or if you just need Jesus—call out to God. Say this prayer:

God, please help me to forgive as you forgive. Give me a heart full of love so that no offense will make its way into my life, but that my heart overlooks offenses. May I look to You, Father. Forgive me of my sins, and please wash me, make me new. I know You sent Your Son to die for me, and for that I thank You. Please come into my life, live with me, direct me, and give me your vision so that I see others the way You see them. Give me a heart that seeks You, and no matter what, please don't ever let me go. With love, my Father, Amen.

To subscribe
to Christina's free blog, go to
ChrisStokesbury.com

Contact Christina at CS@ChrisStokesbury.com

CPSIA information can be obtained at www.ICGtesting.com
Printed in the USA
BVOW08s1301201215

430681BV00001B/81/P